Greenlight
When God Says Go

Dr. Shelly M. Cameron

Copyright © 2018

by

Shelly M. Cameron, EdD

GreenLight: When God Says Go

All rights reserved. No part of this publication may be reproduced, distributed, or transmitted in any form or by any means, including photocopying, recording, or other electronic or mechanical methods, without the prior written permission of the author or publisher, except in the case of brief quotations embodied in critical reviews and certain other noncommercial uses permitted by copyright law.

ISBN: 978-0-692-09749-6

Dr. Cameron, Shelly

www.shellycameron.com

First Printing 2018

Printed in United States of America

Dedicated to my two girls

Monique & Ashleigh

May you remain close to the Lord

This is my prayer

Introduction

I fasted. I prayed. I resigned. I attended a send-off at church. My Pastor's wife Bernice (now deceased) said, "God will guide you on your pilgrimage." My friend Daveyton said it too. "May you be guided on your pilgrimage."

I thought about it. Coincidence? A sign? Not sure. But I decided to trust the Lord and stepped forward in faith to do what He wanted me to do.

How can we know the will of the Lord? It's a question many ask. We never know. But if we pray; if we stay in touch with the Lord; if we tell Him our heart's desires and ask for His guidance in everything, He will guide us through every decision. He will guide us through every step we must take.

Enter GreenLight. I learnt that when we step out in obedience, we can bask in the confidence that God's got our back. He is in control. There are no surprises with Him. The surprises are for us. Sometimes we cry. Sometimes we are confused, and sometimes we jump for joy in praises to His amazing answers! It doesn't have to be mountain moving. Sometimes it's a quiet answer.

Sometimes it's in a still small voice.

I relocated and got involved in Washington DC, United States—the nation's capital. I worked to lend my voice, skills, and talent to community initiatives. I met some amazing people.

But most of all ...I met God. I was a Christian for many years, but I got to *know* my Great, Big, awesome, amazing God! In a new place, you know no one ...all you can do is rely on God. And that's what I did. I spent a year in my closet (before even the mention of the movie War Room); most times in the dark, quiet space, and I talked with God.

After that year, I had finished writing my research and decided to return home to Florida.

This book provides a synopsis of my prayers as I poured out my heart before, during, and after He had said '*Go.*' Sometimes it was a prayer, other times—an exhortation. But most of all, it was my talks and walks with the Lord.

I hope this book of prayers will provide you with the comfort, inspiration, and confidence that you need to step out on your own journey today. Just trust Him. He's Got you!

May you be inspired in some way.

Blessings overflow!

~ Dr. Shelly Cameron

GreenLight

I've always asked God to give me the GREEN LIGHT when I'm driving to work and running late. Whether He does, is not the point. The point is Green Light is like finding out the will of the Lord. We find that out step by step; day by day; walking with Him.

<u>*We cannot get green lights before we're on the road*</u>*; or before we get to the intersections. At the lights, we are told what to do—Prepare to stop; Stop, or Go.*

That's how it is with God's will. When we get to life's intersections (whether it's decision-making, trials, job or career, business, relationships, or other), He tells us what to do, where to go, and what to say. Abraham did it with his son when he said God will provide the lamb to be slaughtered.

Step by step; day by day; with obedience and faith, you too can know God's will for your life.

"Go, eat your food with gladness, and drink your wine with a joyful heart, for God has already approved what you do." (Ecclesiastes 9:7)NIV

Go and I will Tell You What to Do

When God says go, we need to move. Be obedient to His instructions. Step forward in faith. Then He will show His mighty power as He did with men of old.

Peter, when he was told to cast his net on the other side asked, "Lord I am an expert fisherman. What you are asking me to do, does not make sense. It will not work." The Lord answered—try me. In faith, Peter did and could hardly bring in the fish.

In the same way, Cornelius was instructed by God to go, and he would see Saul praying. Me Lord? How can I? Don't you know? Can't you see that this is the man who has been harming the people who speak directly in your name, yet you are asking me to go see him? Well yes, Go to Ananias' house. Then Cornelius stepped out in obedience and went to Ananias' house. There he saw Paul who was immediately healed and went on to become one of the greatest teachers of all times.

Samuel was told to go to the house of Jesse, and he would be told which of his sons to anoint. Lord, how can I do that? If Saul hears about it, he will kill me. The Lord replied, "just go, and I will tell you what to do." Samuel obeyed, went and anointed David who became one of the greatest kings, leader, and writer of many psalms that edify today.

The point is when the Lord speaks—obey. Even when things don't make sense, just obey and watch Him work things out for your good. Remember it's not your plan, it's His! He will work it out!

And we know that all things work together for good to them that love God, to them who are the called according to his purpose. (Romans 8:28)KJV

The Gift

One Christmas, my boss, gave me a gift. It was an envelope. Being the sentimental person that I am, I tucked the envelope away to read later. I love reading and value words. Four months later while going through some stuff on my nightstand, I discovered an envelope. Curious, I opened it wondering why—or if I had forgotten to open it before. Sure enough, I had. When I opened it, there was a Christmas card that had a gift of $100 in it. With a gasp, I immediately called and enquired the reason she had not asked if I had seen it. She just smiled.

It caused me to think. God gives us many valuable gifts packaged in different ways. But if we never open it, we will never receive the value He has in store for us. Why not open your gift today? Accept the value He has for you.

For it is by grace you have been saved, through faith, and this is not from yourselves, it is the gift of God. (Ephesians 2:8) Thanks be to God for His indescribable gift. (2 Corinthians 9:15)

Ask

You have not because you ask not. Why don't you just ask?

Ask and it will be given to you; seek and you will find; knock and the door will be opened to you. For everyone who asks receives; the one who seeks finds; and to the one who knocks, the door will be opened. Which of you, if your son asks for bread, will give him a stone? Or if he asks for a fish, will give him a snake? If you, then, though you are evil, know how to give good gifts to your children, how much more will your Father in heaven give good gifts to those who ask him! (Matthew 7:7-11)NIV

We Forgot to Pray

My grandson RJ awoke with a start and with a loud outburst panicked "We Forgot to Pray!" I replied with a big grin "so let's do it now." To which he replied, "no, it's not night, night."

Caused me to think of how often I 'forget to pray' and when the spirit urges me, I postpone it for the 'right' time. With God, any prayer time is always the right time. What about now?

And pray in the Spirit on all occasions with all kinds of prayers and requests. With this in mind, be alert and always keep on praying for all the saints. (Ephesians 6:18)

Anxious? Don't be

Anxious? Don't be. Just Pray. Give thanks, and you will get the peace that you won't understand.

Be anxious for nothing, but in everything by prayer and supplication, with thanksgiving, let your requests be made known to God; and the peace of God, which surpasses all understanding, will guard your hearts and minds through Christ Jesus. (Philippians 4:6-7)

Almost there

Computer acting up while I was preparing for a presentation. Fed up I said aloud "What is happening Lord?" The immediate response from computer, "*almost there.*"

I applied that response to my heart. To the Lord's action on my prayers, pleadings, and supplication in my life. He said to me, I am "almost there." So, don't worry, just hold on a little while longer.

Thank you, Lord, I have received you comforting reply. I will wait on you. Though I'm getting anxious about the issues that surround me, I know your timing is always right. Forgive my anxiety. Please help me to wait on you.

Jesus told his disciples a story. He wanted to show them that they should always pray and not give up. (Luke 18:1)

Answered Prayer

Thank you, Lord for answering prayers. You did it for me! Now as I start a new chapter, I step forward in obedience knowing that You are by my side and will take care of my every need. I feel joy in my heart. I don't understand it. I know I should be scared but I prayed, and you answered. So, I know You have got this Lord. Thank you, Jesus. Thank you, Lord.

For I know the plans I have for you," declares the Lord, "plans to prosper you and not to harm you, plans to give you hope and a future. (Jeremiah 29:11)

Teaching Someone Instead

Has the Lord ever made you teach and train someone else for a job or opportunity that you yourself wanted? This happened to Moses. No matter how much he pleaded, The Lord had decided he would not set foot on the promised land. Instead, he instructed him to teach and on top of that—encourage Joshua instead.

But before we judge too quickly, Moses prayed, prayed, and prayed ...and the Lord allowed him to see a glimpse of the land He promised the children of Israel.

In the same way, David wanted to build a temple to honor the Lord's name. But the Lord instructed him to teach his son Solomon instead. David prayed, and the Lord allowed him to start the preparation for the building, but he had to teach his son Solomon instead.

May we be encouraged today knowing that the Lord hears and answers our prayers in His way; in His time

But commission Joshua, and encourage and strengthen him, for he will lead this people across and will cause them to inherit the land that you will see. (Deuteronomy 3:28)

Attempt Great things

Attempt Great things for God. Expect Great things from God. King David decided to build a house for the Lord (for the ark of the covenant). But the Lord blessed him instead. Building projects for God are costly. It demands vision, time, sacrifice and perseverance. It all begins with a dream! Do you have a dream of how God may want to use you, your family, skills or resources? Then dream it. Plan it. Pursue it; and as God enables, achieve it.

He does wonderful things that can't be understood. He does miracles that can't even be counted. (Job 5:9)

U-Turns

U-turns—don't you just hate them? It is an inconvenience, but it is necessary especially when we have lost our way and when we need to be on the other side.

It is the same when we must get back on the right track in life when we falter both physically and spiritually. The Lord will be there to guide and direct us.

So even when you're afraid, still make that U-turn. With God's help, you will get right back on track.

You need to persevere so that when you have done the will of God, you will receive what he has promised. (Hebrews 10:36)

Lord You're Amazing

I prayed. Now I wait for Peace that only He can provide. Like He said, watch and be utterly amazed! Lord, you are more than amazing, more than wonderful, more than miraculous, Lord you are everything to me.

Look at the nations and watch— and be utterly amazed. For I am going to do something in your days that you would not believe, even if you were told. (Habakkuk 1:5)

Do Not Tremble. Do Not Be Afraid

May God spring in my life as He did with Job in the latter part of his life. Spring is beautiful.

Say to those whose hearts are afraid, be strong and do not fear. Your God will come. He will pay your enemies back. He will come to save you. (Isaiah 35:14)

Barriers

Lord, tear down all barriers. Remove all fear, doubt, and negative thinking. Grant me peace. Strengthen me. Let me walk in faith. I trust you lord. Let me walk in confidence for I can do all things through you who gives me the strength.

Now I will break Assyria's yoke off your neck. I will tear off the ropes that hold you. (Nahum 1:13)

Bold but Controlled

Lord thank you for giving me that spirit of Wisdom and Boldness. May it always be engulfed with your power and love that leads to my complete self-control!

For the Spirit God gave us does not make us timid, but gives us power, love and self-discipline. (2Timothy 1:7)

Anxiety or Faith: Your Choice

Each day comes with two choices: the choice to approach the day in anxiety, or the choice to approach the day in faith. Lord increase my faith, for I can do all things through Christ.

I was very worried. But your comfort brought me joy. (Psalm 94:19)

God will Complete It

God will complete what He started.

Being confident of this, that he who began a good work in you will carry it on to completion until the day of Christ Jesus. (Philippians 1:6)

Christ-like Response to The Undeserved

Repay evil, manipulation, and negativity with good. Be like Christ.

Don't pay back evil with evil. Don't pay back unkind words with unkind words. Instead, pay back evil with kind words. This is what you have been chosen to do. You will receive a blessing by doing this. (1 Peter 3:9)

Confidence in Life's Storms

Sometimes the Lord calms the storm. More often He lets the storm rage and calms the child. Relax in the Lord. Just relax.

He replied, "Your faith is so small! Why are you so afraid?" Then Jesus got up and ordered the winds and the waves to stop. It became completely calm. (Matthew 8:26)

God Did It!

God did it! King David exclaimed. He used me to burst through my enemies like a raging flood. In faith I wait in anticipation to shout, 'God did it for me.' I cannot do it alone. Oh, just taste and you will see that the Lord is good.

Taste and see that the Lord is good. Blessed is the person who goes to him for safety. (Psalm 34:8)

Encounters with God

During my Seasons of need, the Lord taught me patience, faith, hope, and trust. Above all, I learnt that sometimes He gives us strategies as He did with Joshua when he instructed that they march around the city of Jericho seven times, then give a shout. Sometimes He works miracles to deliver us from difficult situations as He did with the children of Israel, in parting the Red Sea.

I reiterate—all I need is the courage to wait through divine patience; the wisdom to pray, and the faith to trust Him because I am confident of hope. Hope reassures me never to give up because I know He is keeping me even during my human frailties of worry and persistent fear.

The good thing is that even when I am confused, I do not let it stop me. I keep praying and remind Him that I am here waiting and need His help. I need His strength because when I am weak, He is strong. Lord, please give me the courage when I am afraid; when I feel so all alone.

Be strong and brave. Don't be afraid of them. Don't be terrified because of them. The Lord your God will go with you. He will never leave you. He'll never desert you. Then Moses sent for Joshua. Moses spoke to him in front of all the Israelites. He said, Be strong and brave. You must go with these people. They are going into the land the Lord promised to give to their people of long ago. You must divide it up among them. They will each receive their share. The Lord himself will go ahead of you. He will be with you. He will never leave you. He'll never desert you. So, don't be afraid. Don't lose hope. (Deuteronomy 31:6-8).

God's Firm Support

My daughter's 2-year-old son, Xavier, tried climbing onto the bed holding onto a pillow. It's no surprise that he fell backwards. To be sure of completing his climb, he needed a firm foundation. A pillow could not provide that.

How very true of us. How often have we tried to mount the pressures and challenges in life without grasping the firm foundation that only God can provide? May we remember today, to hold onto God's unchanging hand for support. Only then will we be able to deal with life's sure surprises.

He reached down from on high and took hold of me; he drew me out of deep waters. He rescued me from my powerful enemy, from my foes, who were too strong for me. They confronted me in the day of my disaster, but the Lord was my support. He brought me out into a spacious place; he rescued me because he delighted in me. (2 Samuel 22:17-20)

Able to Forgive

I can forgive because Christ forgave me. People do terrible things, but through Christ I can forgive. At times it is hard, and people ask why or how you can forgive. But I have learnt that I can, because of Christ.

In Him we have redemption through his blood, the forgiveness of sins, in accordance with the riches of God's grace that he lavished on us. With all wisdom and understanding, He made known to us the mystery of his will according to His good pleasure, which he purposed in Christ, to be put into effect when the time reach their fulfilment – to bring unity to all things in heaven and on earth under Christ. (Ephesians 1:7-10)

Start to Act Through Faith

I have been reading the Word of God and now realize that He instructs me to act in faith. Hold fast unto His promises knowing that what he says He will do. Just like He did with the descendants of the children of Israel. He told them to cross over into the promised land. Even though the land was already occupied, the place he promised them was not. But He told them to go ahead and prepare.

Start putting things in place because indeed He is coming through. Lord help me today to hold firmly onto your promises knowing that you are coming through for me. And while you are refining me, help me never to give up even in the face of discouragement. Help me to trust you, Lord. To hold onto your firm strong arms for therein lies my one and only true support.

The Lord said to me, See, I have begun to deliver Sihon and his country over to you. Now begin to conquer and possess his land. (Deuteronomy 2:31)

Grace

Thank you, Lord for the grace to walk the difficult road of life. May Grace overflow like the strongest rope to get me through when the going gets tough.

But he said to me, "My grace is sufficient for you, for my power is made perfect in weakness." Therefore, I will boast all the more gladly about my weaknesses, so that Christ's power may rest on me. (2 Corinthians 12:9)

Learning from the Wise—Ants

I remember watching ants while praying. Saw some ants in the room walking on a trail. But unknown to them my shoe was in the corner. Now to ants, my shoe is like a huge mountain. So, I sat there watching them. I could move it or watch to see what they would do. How they would handle it.

It's the same with our great big awesome God. He sees what's ahead of us and will help us if only we ask Him. He can move mountains. Oh yes, He can...but first, we must ask.

Please Lord, remind me always to ask; to always speak with you.

If you believe, you will receive whatever you ask for in prayer. (Matthew 21:22)

God Answered Before

God answered before. He will answer again.

The vision is for an appointed time. It will surely come, it will not tarry. Wait for it. (Habakkuk 2:3)

Jacob

I love Joseph! His brothers were mean to him. They sold him as a slave. But God had a plan. My focus was always on Joseph and how he loved and trusted the Lord. It meant everything to me throughout my life. Then a bible study that I attended opened my eyes to Jacob—Joseph's dad; the mean guy. Jacob the deceiver. I actually disliked him most of my life. Why? He deceived his father and brother Esau in getting his birthright.

But later in life when he was old and grey, he longed for his son Joseph who he thought had died because his other sons had told him so.

Then, when the Lord finally opened the doors for Joseph, and he was in charge in Egypt, Jacob was asked to visit. But he was afraid. He didn't want to lose his youngest son.

I never thought much about Jacob, who was a deceiver in his early life, yet was himself deceived by his father-in-law years later. He had to work 14 years to get Joseph's mom, Rachel. No wonder he loved Joseph so much.

The point is, Jacob was afraid to go to Egypt because he could not see the future. Yet, God had a plan! When he finally gave in and went, he not only received back his youngest son, Benjamin; he also received back to life, his other son Joseph! Oh, how the Lord works if we only trust Him!

I walked away from that study thinking of how scared I am at times because I cannot see what's around the corner. I can't see what lies ahead. But through Jacob's experience, my mind has been rekindled to trust the Lord who holds the future.

When you can't see, obey and trust Him. He will work it out.

The Lord Almighty is with us; the God of Jacob is our fortress. (Psalm 46:11)

Believe

Pray, believe, receive the answers to your prayers.

So, I tell you, when you pray for something, believe that you have already received it. Then it will be yours. (Mark 11:24)

It's Morning!

My daughter's 5-year-old son, RJ, ran into the kitchen where I was and shouted "it's morning! Thank you, God, it's finally morning!!" He was awake most of the night unable to fall back asleep after a weird dream. When he finally fell back asleep, he didn't realize that the sun had finally come out 2 hours before. He was overjoyed!

How often our lives feel like the night will never end. Things feel gloomy, and no matter what we do, life never seems to change. But the bible teaches that joy comes in the morning. The morning will come. Let's Take our nightly concerns to the only one who can change things.

Weeping may endure for a night, but joy cometh in the morning (Psalm 30:5).

I Sought. He Heard.

Lord, you always answer when I seek you through your Word. You have never failed me when I seek you. I know I can trust that your word is always right. Oh, what a relief it is to know that you always answer.

I sought The Lord and He heard and answered my prayers. I looked to the Lord, and he answered me. He saved me from everything I was afraid of. (Psalm 34:4)

Ask. Seek. Knock

Ask, and it will be given. Seek, and you will find. Knock on doors of the potential, and the doors will be opened.

Ask and it will be given to you; seek and you will find; knock and the door will be opened to you. For everyone who asks receives; the one who seeks finds; and to the one who knocks, the door will be opened. (Matthew 7:7-8)

Wait: God is About to Answer

Waiting on the Lord to answer. I feel His answer coming through. I feel like I am in labor pain and about to give birth—to deliver. Lord, I feel it. Lord help me to wait in expectancy quietly. Help me –Push. Help me ease the birthing pain. Help me.

I can Do All Things through Christ. (Proverbs 3:5)

Help Me

With all my heart I wait for the Lord to help me. I put my hope in his word. I wait for the Lord to help me. I wait with more longing than those on guard duty wait for the morning. I'll say it again. I wait with more longing than those on guard duty wait for the morning.

Israel, put your hope in the Lord, because the Lord's love never fails. He sets his people completely free. He himself will set Israel free from all their sins. (Psalm 130:7)

I Am Too Young

Don't Be Afraid "The word of the Lord came to me, saying, "Before I formed you in the womb I knew you, before you were born I set you apart; I appointed you as a prophet to the nations."

"Alas, Sovereign Lord," I said, "I do not know how to speak; I am too young." But the Lord said to me, "Do not say, 'I am too young.' You must go to everyone I send you to and say whatever I command you. Do not be afraid of them, for I am with you and will rescue you," declares the Lord." (Jeremiah 1:4-8)

Pray Before You Answer

I prayed, then I answered. Always pray before you answer. God is available every hour, every minute, especially during important conversations and life-changing events.

The king said to me, "What do you want?" I prayed to the God of heaven. Then I answered king, are you pleased with me, King Artaxerxes? If it pleases you, send me to Judah. Let me go to the city of Jerusalem. That's where my people are buried. I want to rebuild it. May I also have a letter to Asaph? He takes care of your forest. I want him to give me some logs so I can make beams out of them. I want to use them for the gates of the fort that is by the temple. Some of the logs will be used in the city wall. And I'll need some for the house I'm going to live in. The gracious hand of God helped me. So, the king gave me what I asked for (Nehemiah 2:4,5 & 8)

On Bended Knees

Here I am Lord, on bended knees I come. Please take care of me.

The Lord is good. When people are in trouble, they can go to him for safety. He takes good care of those who trust in him. (Nahum 1:7)

Kneel. Pray. Wait

Kneel and pray while you wait. The Lord is almost there. Remember His timing is perfect. "Help me, O Lord, to be content! My lips to seal, to every vain desire, each whim—instead to kneel, acknowledging Thee, Lord and King, and in that place, to kneel, to pray, to wait until I see Thy face! —Adams (extracted from Daily Bread)

Rejoice always, pray continually, give thanks in all circumstances; for this is God's will for you in Christ Jesus. (1 Thessalonians 5:16-18)

Decision-Making

Before making a decision, be wise. Seek Counsel, and you will accomplish the will of God. Only then will your plans Succeed.

"Plans go wrong for lack of advice; many advisers bring success. (Proverbs 15:22)

The Lord Heard

Thank you Lord, that you have heard my cries and pleas for help. Please continue to work the process through to the end because it's never over until it's over. Lord keep me faithful even after it's done. I love you, Jesus. I love you, Lord.

If you remain in me and my words remain in you, ask whatever you wish, and it will be done for you. (John 15:7)

But God

When you feel discouraged, remember God is always there. It's simple. When the discouragement comes, remember; but God. When the bills, the pain, the job—but God. When we yearn for our kids, our friends and family—remember, but God. He remains the strength of our heart.

My flesh and my heart may fail, But God is the strength of my heart and my portion forever. (Psalm 73:26)

Blessings

Lord, we praise you for your blessings, and we cry for your intervention in the affairs of our lives and that of our nations worldwide.

I urge, then, first of all, that petitions, prayers, intercession and thanksgiving be made for all people. (1 Timothy 2:1)

I Will Bless You ...Again

I will make you into a great nation. I will bless you. I will make your name great. You will be a blessing to others. I will bless those who bless you. I will put a curse on anyone who calls down a curse on you. God will take care of everything you need.

*All nations on earth will be blessed because of you."
(Genesis 12:2, 3)*

The Battle

The battle is not yours—it is the Lord's. I told you to make that move, so don't worry I will take care of things. Just leave it to me. Haven't I already taken care of the other things?

Do not be afraid or troubled because of these many men. For the battle is not yours but God's. (2 Chronicles 20:15)

God's Blessings

God's abundant blessings. So undeserved. Yet, we are wise to accept.

And God said to him, 'I am God Almighty; be fruitful and increase in number. A nation and a community of nations will come from you, and kings will be among your descendants. The land I gave to Abraham and Isaac I also give to you, and I will give this land to your descendants after you. (Genesis 35-11-12)

New Beginnings

In the Beginning –GOD. He will help us with our new beginnings when we need to start over.

Your beginnings will seem humble, so prosperous will your future be. (Job 8:7)

Life Renewed

Behold I am doing a new thing. Do you not perceive it?

Thank you, Lord, for your guidance, direction and showing me the opportunities that exist. God is doing a new thing in my life and my loved ones too. I must let go of my past. It's no longer "*what I did back the*n" but to be open to what God is doing in my life right here, right now.

Forget the things that happened in the past. Do not keep on thinking about them. I am about to do something new. It is beginning to happen even now. Don't you see it coming? I am going to make a way for you to go through the desert. I will make streams of water in the dry and empty land. (Isaiah 43:18, 19)

The End is Better Than the Beginning

Be Brave. Be Strong. Be on your guard. Stand firm in the faith.

The end of a matter is better than its beginning, and patience is better than pride. (Ecclesiastes 7:8)

God's Blessings

May the Lord bless you and take good care of you.

The Lord bless you and keep you; the Lord make his face shine on you and be gracious to you; the Lord turn his face toward you and give you peace (Numbers 6:24-26)

Call, He will Answer

Feeling down and out with your cares and troubles? Call on the name of the Lord. He will answer you.

He will call on me, and I will answer him; I will be with him in trouble, I will deliver him and honor him. (Psalm 91:15)

His Leading

God's Assurance of His rescue.

The word of the Lord came to me, saying, "Before I formed you in the womb I knew you, before you were born I set you apart; I appointed you as a prophet to the nations." "Alas, Sovereign Lord," I said, "I do not know how to speak; I am too young." But the Lord said to me, "Do not say, 'I am too young.' You must go to everyone I send you to and say whatever I command you. Do not be afraid of them, for I am with you and will rescue you," declares the Lord.

God's Call

God calls us at any time, any age, anyhow. We just need to respond, be obedient and act according to His will. In this way, we will accomplish his plan and purpose for our life. Thank you, Jesus, for calling me. Please help me to honor and respond so I may achieve your will and purpose for my life.

When Abram was ninety-nine years old, the Lord appeared to him and said, "I am God Almighty; walk before me faithfully and be blameless." (Genesis 17:1)

Changes: God's Control

Our God is in control of our every situation. These simple prayers show. Lord, why have you forsaken me? Prayer answered in your way Lord to relieve my stress. Now I must build my trust in the future because even though you had forsaken Christ on the cross, you will never leave me because Jesus paid it all.

Father, into your hand I commit my future; Steer, direct, guide and help me in this time of need. Lord, I thirst for you. Please grant me the peace that you will take care of all my needs.

It is finished. The end of that crazy stressful era marks the start of a new chapter; a new race. A life entirely devoted to accomplishing the will of the Lord. Where do I go from here? I'm not sure, but I do know that God remains in control. All I need is for you Lord to hold me not only by my right hand but also my left. Lead me, guide me, and lift me over this hurdle as only you can. And as I do it, I pray for peace in the midst of this storm. Peace not only to me but for my family. Hear this my prayer. Answer me, Lord. Surprise me, Lord, as only you can. Thank you, Jesus. Thank you, Lord.

When he had received the drink, Jesus said, "It is finished." (John 19:30)

Our Stuff

Often our 'stuff' in this life gets in the way of our fellowship, and followership with the Lord. I am reminded of His request, "Choose today who you will serve." Today, I pray that I will have the right focus and choose to serve the Lord with my whole heart and my whole being. Lord, help me. When I'm weak, make me strong.

Jesus looked at him and loved him. "One thing you lack," he said. "Go, sell everything you have and give to the poor, and you will have treasure in heaven. Then come, follow me." (Mark 10:21)

My Counselor

The Lord is my counselor. Even at night, He counsels me.

I will praise the Lord, who counsels me; even at night my heart instructs me. (Psalm 16:7)

In the Beginning God

In the beginning, God created my goal, and my thoughts were without form and void; and God said, let "there be light"; and my goal became alive.

Lord, in my weakness, please strengthen me. Help me to do all things only through you who gives me strength. Breathe in me and help me not to fear, for I know you will take care of me.

And God said, "Let there be light," and there was light. (Genesis 1:3)

Stop Busyness and Listen

Lord in the busyness of my life, help me to stop and listen to you. Help me always to focus on You.

"But one thing is necessary. Mary has chosen the good portion, which will not be taken away from her." (Luke 10:42)

Crisis Prayer

Crisis prayer. Emergency prayer. God answers still. But Breathed prayers offer the sweetest return. They are the prayers that are offered to our Lord. As Christian Hurst explained, the best prayer happens in the attitude of a conversation. Let your prayer be a conversation with the Lord.

And pray in the Spirit on all occasions with all kinds of prayers and requests. With this in mind, be alert and always keep on praying for all the Lord's people. (Ephesians 6:18)

Celebrate! Rejoice as You Progress

We are to Praise the Lord, celebrate achievements as we progress doing the everyday things in life. David recruited builders, supervisors, gatekeepers and he also recruited men to praise the Lord on musical instruments while they worked. Lord may I be like David and always Praise you as I work.

Four thousand are to be gatekeepers and four thousand are to praise the Lord with the musical instruments I have provided for that purpose. (1 Chronicles 23:5)

Confused

My child said mommy "I'm not really disappointed in The Lord, I am just confused. I'm not sure what He's doing, or what He wants me to do."

My observation. She's shy, alone, and the little hope she had—diminished. Lord, please give us wisdom, knowledge and the understanding of what your expectations are, and help us in and through your strength to meet them. Lord, we know that we can do all things through you.

So, as we continue to wait these many months, may we never grow tired and weary. May we lean only on you with the confidence that this too shall pass and be always comforted knowing that all things work together for good to those who love the Lord. So, Lord, please strengthen, guide, protect and give us patience and peace while we wait.

Be patient, then, brothers and sisters, until the Lord's coming. See how the farmer waits for the land to yield its valuable crop, patiently waiting for the autumn and spring rains. You too, be patient and stand firm. (James 5:7-8).

Provisions in Life's Desert

Can God put food on a table in the desert? Oh yes, He can, and He did! He gave the Israelites water from the rock to quench their thirst and manna from heaven. They ate until they were satisfied.

Why don't we trust God more? So many evidence of His mighty power exists in our lives and all around us. Lord help my unbelief. Strengthen my trust as I wait on you.

"They spoke against God. They said, "Can God put food on a table in the desert?" (Psalm 78:19)

Counterintuitive

God's ways are not our ways. I think of hurricane Mathew and the path it took—meandering, unpredictable. Countries prepared for its wreck, yet it swerved aside some and devastated others.

Personally, I asked for time to finish up a personal goal that was lagging. At the beginning of the week, I was sad. Didn't have the time to do what I needed. Then came the hurricane threat. All the activities that I was involved with that demanded my time were canceled, giving me time.

Naturally, work subsequently closed giving me even more time to work while we waited for the storm. Then a conference I was expected to attend was canceled giving me my entire weekend to work.

Lord, you are amazing. Please route me to you always to pray. Help me to put my needs before you with the confidence that you will work things out for my ultimate good. Indeed, Lord, you do more than we can ask, dream, or think. Your ways are not our ways. Help me Lord God to always trust you.

Today, I encourage you to consider what these counterintuitive principles from the Bible might mean to you.

"Whoever loses their life for me will find it" (Matt. 16:25). "The last will be first, and the first will be last" (Matt. 20:16). "When I am weak, then I am strong" (2 Cor. 12:10). God chose the foolish things of the world to shame the wise. (1 Corinthians 1:27)

Discernment

Any time you face a major decision, opportunity, or crisis, you turn to God's word for God's wisdom. Ask Him to guide you. Moreover, open your heart and ask the Holy Spirit to teach, show, lead, and guide you.

Lord please direct my reading and studying. I want to know your highest and best for my life.

He speaks in a still, small voice (1 Kings 1912). Teach me good judgment and knowledge (Psalm 119:66)

My Desert Place

Be careful of your thoughts. When I moved away from my birthplace in the Caribbean, I said I was going to my desert place to attain success; to be the best that I could be. But the desert is a place that has trials, hardships, discomforts and more. My experience molded and made me into what Christ wants me to be.

Adherence to hardship makes us endure to achieve greatness in order to achieve our full potential in Christ. In the desert is where God positions us to be a blessing to others.

Circumstances allowed by God shaped me into becoming a spiritual character of substance. I hate the circumstances, but I love the end-product. I am being molded by my God into what He desires.

Yet you Lord, are our Father. We are the clay, you are the potter; we are all the work of your hand. (Isaiah 64:8)

Doubting Thomas

Don't be a doubting Thomas. There is a story of a lady who lost her young son to cancer. She worked long and hard to care for him, and when he died, she was devastated. She stopped doing everything to this day.

The same thing happened with the character, Miss Havisham from the novel *Great Expectations*. Her groom left her at the altar. She remained in her gown for the rest of her life. Oh, how much she missed.

Difficult times are hard. When life becomes difficult, keep strong. Hold firmly to the lord. Don't be a doubting Thomas. Trust God today and always, even when things go awry.

Then he said to Thomas, "Put your finger here; see my hands. Reach out your hand and put it into my side. Stop doubting and believe." Thomas said to him, "My Lord and my God!" (John 20:27-28)

Dreams

Do what you can, and God will do what you can't. Be prepared. Get ready to be propelled forward.

It is pleasant to see dreams come true, but fools refuse to turn from evil to attain them. (Proverbs 13:19)

Distance Hurts

Distance hurts. When loved ones and parents are afar and illness steps in, we can turn to God who alone can bridge the gap.

God is our place of safety. He gives us strength. He is always there to help us in times of trouble. (Psalm 46:1)

Easier Said Than Done

Things are easier said than done. But I am confident that I can do all things through Christ who gives me strength. Because He is able to do exceedingly abundantly above all I could ever ask or think, and for that I thank Him.

I can do all this through him who gives me strength (Philippians 4:13)

Evil

Often it seems evil, and people who do wrong succeed. But they won't last long because God is still in charge and will be victorious.

Those who are evil spring up like grass. Those who do wrong succeed. But they will be destroyed forever. (Psalm 92:7)

Enemies

The year ahead. In faith, you will work in my life Lord. In faith I commit my fears, my thoughts, my goals, and my aspirations to you. And right after that in faith I know you will bring the joys and success to my family.

Right in front of my enemies. You prepare a feast for me right in front of my enemies. You pour oil on my head. My cup runs over. (Psalm 23:5)

Experience Is Important

While doing an *Experiencing God* class, I received the revelation that I should write in a book everything I see. I subsequently published a book on Success Strategies. But the Lord inspired me to write this book titled Greenlight.

I was inspired by a speaker and received the revelation that to write; I need to 'see' and experience things along the way. So, it has now brought a new perspective on the things I have experienced with God. I am now more able to "write what I see."

The Lord replied, write down the message I am giving you. Write it clearly on the tablets you use. Then a messenger can read it and run to announce it. (Habakkuk 2;2)

Faith

By faith we believe; by faith Abel offered a better sacrifice; by faith Enoch was taken up; by faith Noah constructed an ark; by faith Abraham went to the Promised Land when he did not know where he was going; by faith Sarah received power to conceive which led to descendants more than sands on seashore.

By faith, Moses was hidden and in the end, achieved much for the sake of the Lord—the invisible one. By faith the people crossed the Red Sea; by faith David, Samson, Rahab, Samuel... all achieved God's purpose and promise. We will too, but only if we believe—even when things do not make sense.

*Now faith is the substance if things hoped for, the evidence if things not seen. (Hebrews **11:1**)*

Be Patient

Disappointment is just God's way of saying I have something better. Be patient; have faith; wait. Trust the Lord. His timing is always perfect because He plans to do more than we could ever ask or think.

Let us continue to ask God to strengthen our faith while we wait—at times even impatiently on Him. He always knows best.

So, Jacob worked for seven years so he could marry Rachel. But they seemed like only a few days to him because he loved her so much. (Genesis 29:20)

Faithfulness

Thank you, Lord for remaining faithful. Your mercies are new every morning. Great is thy faithfulness.

The Lord loves us very much. So we haven't been completely destroyed. His loving concern never fails. His great love is new every morning. Lord, how faithful you are. (Lamentations 3:22-23)

Do Not Fret

Do not fret. It leads only to evil. As a friend reminded, be confident that in faith, it will happen. Hope anticipates with optimism, but with the Lord's help, it will come to pass.

"Be strong and courageous. Do not be afraid or discouraged because of the king of Assyria and the vast army with him, for there is a greater power with us than with him. (2 Chronicles 32:7)

Feelings

Life is not about Feelings. Feelings misinform. When the storms of life hit as they always do, you feel sad, down, distraught. But then you bask in the comfort that God is with you in the midst of the storm.

Be still my heart, for The Lord is my God. He sees every pain, every heartache, every tear. He knows when you are at your wit's end and unable to do anything more. That's when He takes over the reign. So be still my heart for the Lord is my God. He is coming through. He never leaves you. He is always there.

So be still. Be confident. Stay in trust. Hold on. Don't Give up. Restoration is just around the corner.

He says, "Be still, and know that I am God; I will be exalted among the nations, I will be exalted in the earth." (Psalms 46:10)

Favor

Remember me with favor oh God. Grant it as only you can.

Be careful that no one tempts you with riches. Don't take money from people who want special favors, no matter how much it is. (Job 36:18)

Have Faith in the Lord Your God

Have faith in the Lord your God, and you will be successful. He will fight the battle for you. Don't worry, just pray, then go out and fight in his strength. He will do it for you. For the battle is not yours but the Lord's. I have seen him do it and He will do it again.

He said listen, King Jehoshaphat and all who live in Judah and Jerusalem! This is what the Lord says to you: 'Do not be afraid or discouraged because of this vast army. For the battle is not yours, but God's. Tomorrow march down against them. They will be climbing up by the Path of Ziz, and you will find them at the end of the gorge in the Desert of Jeruel. You will not have to fight this battle. Take up your positions; stand firm and see the deliverance the Lord will give you, Judah and Jerusalem. Do not be afraid; do not be discouraged. Go out to face them tomorrow, and the Lord will be with you. Jehoshaphat bowed down with his face to the ground, and all the people of Judah and Jerusalem fell down in worship before the Lord. Then some Levites from the Kohathites and Korahites stood up and praised the Lord, the God of Israel, with a very loud voice. Early in the morning they left for the Desert of Tekoa. As they set out, Jehoshaphat stood and said, "Listen to me, Judah and people of Jerusalem! Have faith in the Lord your God and you will be upheld; have faith in his prophets and you will be successful." After consulting the people, Jehoshaphat appointed men to sing to the Lord and to praise him for the splendor of his holiness as they went out at the head of the army, saying: "Give thanks to the Lord, for his love endures forever." As they began to sing and praise, the Lord set ambushes against the men of Ammon and Moab and Mount Seir who were invading Judah, and they were defeated. (2 Chronicles 20:15-22)

Walk by Faith

We walk by faith, but we stand on fact. The fact that what the Lord has said He will do. He always does.

From of old as in the case of his promised son that was sent, the sending of the Holy Spirit, the resurrection, the raising of Lazarus and my all-time favorite the parting of the Red Sea! To this day when He continues His miracles providing the basic needs of life—food, shelter, family, love, encouragement, much more. My God continues to provide. He does exceedingly more than I can ever imagine or dream of. Thank you, Jesus. Thank you, Lord.

For we walk by faith; not by sight. (2 Corinthians 5:7)

Fear

Feel the Fear and do it anyway. "I can't lose—regardless of the outcome of the decision I make. The world is a place for opportunity, and I look forward to the opportunities for learning and growing that either pathway gives me" - Susan Jeffers

For I am the Lord, your God, who takes hold of your right hand and says to you, do not fear; I will help you. (Isaiah 41:13 NIVUK)

Friendship

"Friendship improves happiness and abates misery, by the doubling of our joy and the dividing of our grief."

Brothers and sisters, in all our trouble and suffering your faith cheered us up. Now we really live, because you are standing firm in the Lord. (1 Thessalonians 3:7- 8)

Fasting

The purpose of fasting is to undo heavy burdens, to seek clarity in direction and decision-making.

"Shout it aloud, do not hold back. Raise your voice like a trumpet. Declare to my people their rebellion and to the house of Jacob their sins. For day after day they seek me out; they seem eager to know my ways, as if they were a nation that does what is right and has not forsaken the commands of its God. They ask me for just decisions and seem eager for God to come near them. 'Why have we fasted,' they say, 'and you have not seen it? Why have we humbled ourselves, and you have not noticed?' "Yet on the day of your fasting, you do as you please and exploit all your workers. Your fasting ends in quarrelling and strife, and in striking each other with wicked fists. You cannot fast as you do today and expect your voice to be heard on high. Is this the kind of fast I have chosen, only a day for a man to humble himself? Is it only for bowing one's head like a reed and for lying on sackcloth and ashes? Is that what you call a fast, a day acceptable to the Lord? "Is not this the kind of fasting I have chosen: to loosen the chains of injustice and untie the cords of the yoke, to set the oppressed free and break every yoke? Is it not to share your food with the hungry and to provide the poor wanderer with shelter- when you see the naked, to clothe him, and not to turn away from your own flesh and blood? Then your light will break forth like the dawn, and your healing will quickly appear; then your righteousness will go before you, and the glory of the Lord will be your rear guard. Then you will call, and the Lord will answer; you will cry for help,

and he will say: Here am I. "If you do away with the yoke of oppression, with the pointing finger and malicious talk, and if you spend yourselves on behalf of the hungry and satisfy the needs of the oppressed, then your light will rise in the darkness, and your night will become like the noonday. The Lord will guide you always; he will satisfy your needs in a sun-scorched land and will strengthen your frame. You will be like a well-watered garden, like a spring whose waters never fail. Your people will rebuild the ancient ruins and will raise up the age-old foundations; you will be called Repairer of Broken Walls, Restorer of Streets with Dwellings. (Isaiah 58:1-12)

God's Promise of Deliverance

If you stay, I will build you up and not tear you down. As I said in my word, I will plant you and not uproot you for I have relented concerning the disaster I inflicted on you since its purpose was that you grow in strength and to develop you.

So, do not be afraid of the King of your circumstances, for I am with you, and will keep and deliver you from their hands.

If you stay in this land, I will build you up and not tear you down; I will plant you and not uproot you, for I have relented concerning the disaster I have inflicted on you. Do not be afraid of the king of Babylon, whom you now fear. Do not be afraid of him, declares the Lord, for I am with you and will save you and deliver you from his hands. (Jeremiah 42:10-11).

Healing

Father God I place my friends in your hands. I thank you for the decision to be with their mom and dad at this time. Lord, I place in your hands the terrible sickness that has come upon them. Come quickly Lord and heal them. Lord, may they have more good days than bad. Lord may they experience the beauty of your peace in their minds. We place this situation before you and ask for your peace, love, and comfort. Thank you, Lord for your answer.

Yet when they were ill, I put on sackcloth and humbled myself with fasting. When my prayers returned to me unanswered, I went about mourning as though for my friend or brother. I bowed my head in grief as though weeping for my mother. (Psalm 35:13-14).

Hope

The Lord has placed the word hope in my heart. Because when we have hope we can go on. God remains in charge of our lives. In faith, we can go on because we trust in Him.

Trust in the Lord with all your heart. (Proverbs 3:5)

Rough Day at Work

There will sometimes be rough days at work. So hang in there. Breathe. Take things one step at a time. Walk away when you need to. Then return and continue. Keep your mind on pleasant thoughts—on whatever brings you smiles. Then have a perfect day with God's help.

God is our refuge and strength, an ever-present help in trouble. Therefore, we will not fear, though the earth gives way and the mountains fall into the heart of the sea, though its waters roar and foam and the mountains quake with their surging. (Psalm 46:1-3)

Gentle Jesus

Gentle Jesus meek and mild, look upon a little child. Lord the older I get, the more I depend on you. Thank you for always being there.

People were bringing little children to Jesus for him to place his hands on them, but the disciples rebuked them. When Jesus saw this, he was indignant. He said to them, "Let the little children come to me, and do not hinder them, for the kingdom of God belongs to such as these. Truly I tell you, anyone who will not receive the kingdom of God like a little child will never enter it." And he took the children in his arms, placed his hands on them and blessed them (Mark 10:13-16)

Launch Out into The Unknown

Experiencing discomfort post-emergency surgery, the lady behind me at church noticed my discomfort. She rubbed my shoulder and whispered in my ear, "God's Gonna Fix it." Later, Joel Osteen in his sermon said if you are going to walk on water, you have to get out of the boat! So, I am getting out of the boat.

Years ago, I was obedient. I prayed, and I fasted. Then I followed what I knew was the Lord's leading. I launched out into the deep, left the comfort of the familiar friends, family, and environment behind, then went to a strange place. I experienced discomfort. I also experienced the excitement of launching out into the unknown. I excelled. Moving in obedience to the will of the Lord, I got closer to Him through experiencing immense need (yikes!). Though I hated that period of want and need, it forced me to develop a closer walk with the Lord. I lived in total dependence on Him for everything.

But at the end of it all, I needed to step out of the boat (launched out, now step out) so that I can walk on water. No human can walk on water without God's divine intervention. But I must continue my quest of obedience to step out to achieve my full potential and embrace what He has in store for me. To accomplish His will through the blessing I hopefully can be to others through bringing the Lord's will for me, to life. Thank you, Lord for continuing to hold me strong and in your way "fix my life" so I can accomplish your will and purpose.

When he had finished speaking, he said to Simon, "Put out into deep water, and let down the nets for a catch. (Luke 5:14)

Keep the Faith

Keep the faith. Keep praying. Keep trusting. God has already spoken to the right people to help you. Just like He did with Moab who spoke with his workers to help Ruth (even without talking directly to her). He did this before through many others to grant you favor. Just keep holding on. He's coming through for you.

For My thoughts are not your thoughts, nor are your ways My ways," says the Lord. (Isaiah 55:8)

God has been Gracious

I have always been proud (so they say). And yes, I must admit there is some truth to it. I like to give but am always hesitant to ask for help or to accept the gifts that others offer. But I was 'scolded' by a friend who said that I should never stop her from receiving God's blessings. Since then I have learnt to accept what the Lord sends through others. It's not on my terms, but His.

Please accept the present that was brought to you, for God has been gracious to me and I have all I need." And because Jacob insisted, Esau accepted it. (Genesis 33:11)

GOALS

Is Anything too hard? No, nothing is too hard for the Lord. His word says it, and we can believe it.

"I am the Lord, the God of all mankind. Is anything too hard for me? (Jeremiah 32:27)

Don't Look Back

Don't look back. Keep plodding. Let go and let God have His way.

Jesus replied, "Suppose you start to plow and then look back. If you do, you are not fit for service in God's kingdom." (Luke 9:62)

Guidance

One of the great joys and challenges of life is to look expectantly for the hand of God in all of life's circumstances. The Lord is always near. He is behind us and before us and God never sends you where He has not been

All things work together for good to those who love the Lord and are called according to His purpose. (Romans 8:28)

God Heard

They cried out for help, and God heard. He looked down and knew it was time to act. As you cry to God for help, know that He has heard you and is ready to help. Remember as Yolanda Adams sang, *"it's your time... go get your blessing."*

Then you will call on me and come and pray to me, and I will listen to you. (Jeremiah 29:12)

Go

You won't know unless you go. You have no idea of how Jesus is going to use you unless you go and do what He says you need to do.

Go wherever I send you and say whatever I command 'Alas, Sovereign Lord,' I said, 'I do not know how to speak; I am too young.' But the Lord said to me, 'Do not say, "I am too young." You must go to everyone I send you to and say whatever I command you. Do not be afraid of them, for I am with you and will rescue you,' declares the Lord. (Jeremiah 1:6-8)

Eyes Fixed on God

Lord help me to keep my eyes fixed on you for guidance, leadership, and direction in my life.

Fixing our eyes on Jesus, the pioneer and perfecter of faith. For the joy set before him he endured the cross, scorning its shame, and sat down at the right hand of the throne of God. (Hebrews 12:2)

Grace

Thank you, Lord for the grace to walk the difficult road of life. May Grace overflow like the strongest rope to get me through when the going gets tough.

But to each one of us grace has been given as Christ apportioned it. (Ephesians 4:7)

God's Sure Delivery

Shall I bring you to the point of birth and not cause you to bring forth?

Shall I, who cause to bring forth, shut the womb? says your God. (Isaiah 66:9)

God's Got You

Sometimes God goes before us. Other times He protects us from behind. He is greater than any of the forces around us. He did this with the children of Israel, and He will do it for you and me if we only ask—if we only seek Him. He's got you.

The angel of God had been traveling in front of Israel's army. Now he moved back and went behind them. The pillar of cloud also moved away from in front of them. Now it stood behind them. (Exodus 14:19)

For Your Good

If you know that all things work together for good to those who love the Lord; and if you know that the Lord is keeping you, then what are you worrying about? All you need to do is encourage yourself to trust in the Lord with all your heart. If things seem confusing, do not try to rely on your own understanding. Just remember in everything you plan to do, talk to Him beforehand. Let Him know, and He will direct you where to go, what to do, and what to say.

But if it is from God, you will not be able to overthrow them. You may even find yourselves fighting against God. (Acts 5:39)

Help

Hold on; help is on the way.

Lead me, Oh Lord, in your righteousness because of my enemies. Make straight your way before me. (Psalm 5:8)

How Can I Say Thanks?

In response to answered prayer I pondered—how can I say thanks for the things you have done for me, Lord? Things so undeserved yet you provided for me. I just want to praise you, Lord.

Give thanks to the Lord, for he is good; his love endures forever. (1Chronicles 16:34)

Heads Up! All Eyes on Jesus

Lord help me to keep my eyes, heart, and my whole being focused on you. Remove distractions of things loved, social media distraction, the cares of this world, bills, and any idols that may steal the time I need to spend with you. Thank you, Jesus.

Since, then, you have been raised with Christ, set your hearts on things above, where Christ is, seated at the right hand of God." (Colossians 3:1)

Faith, Hope, and Trust

Faith. Hope. Trust. God will make a way—and He did. I have Hope because of my Faith in God. I know I can Trust Him because I know He has got me.

Have I not commanded you? Be strong and courageous. Do not be afraid, for the Lord your God will be with you wherever you go. (Joshua 1:9)

Fear but Faith

Jesus on the night when He was going to be betrayed, prayed in anguish. This makes me realize how much He understands our human frailties. He was God! But when He came, He was like us. I am comforted in that knowledge. He died not an instant death but through immense suffering. Even then in the midst of fear, He showed immense faith. Lord help me be strong. In the midst of my fears, increase my faith.

And being in anguish, he prayed more earnestly, and his sweat was like drops of blood falling to the ground." Luke 22:44

Are You There?

Why have you forsaken me, Lord? Are you there? Are you seeing what's happening? Please don't ignore me. Please show me the way I should go. Please guide, direct, and clear the path for me. For I am up to my neck in fear. The enemy seeks to devour my flesh. I am afraid. Grant me favor Lord as only you can. Why have you forsaken me? These were the words uttered by you lord Jesus when you were on the cross. So, I know you understand how it feels. Thank you for interceding and clearing the path for me. Thank you for your answer to this my prayer.

About three in the afternoon Jesus cried out in a loud voice, "Eli, Eli, lema sabachthani?" (which means "My God, my God, why have you forsaken me?"). (Matthew 27:46)

Pride

He Takes away your pride, so you can learn that things will go well.

"He gave you manna to eat in the desert. Your parents had never even known anything about manna before. The Lord took your pride away. He put you to the test. He did it so that things would go well with you in the end."
(Deuteronomy 8:16)

Help

Lord Help. When life knocks you down, you're in the perfect position to pray. Lord, please help. Please intervene today. You know my needs, my wants my weaknesses, my fears. Lord, please have mercy on me today. Thank you for your strength and for giving me the will and power to persist. I can only do it through you who gives me the strength. In Jesus name. Amen

Let us then approach God's throne of grace with confidence, so that we may receive mercy and find grace to help us in our time of need." (Hebrews 4:16)

Self-Care

It's important to take time out to rest.

Jesus said to them, `Come away with me. Let us go alone to a quiet place and rest for a while.' Many people were coming and going. They could not even eat. (Mark 6:31)

Just Be Still

Amidst all the hustle and bustle of my life, my fears, concerns, and insecurities; all I've heard through scripture is be still. Be still and know that I am God. I will be exalted among the nations through what I'm going to do through you. The Lord will fight for you. Just be still. Trust Him. Have Faith. Hold onto Hope. He's coming through.

Be still before the Lord and wait patiently for him; do not fret when people succeed in their ways, when they carry out their wicked schemes." (Psalm 37:7)

Kneel

When life gives you more than you can stand—Kneel. Fight the good fight on your knees.

For this reason, I kneel before the Father, from whom every family in heaven and on earth derives its name. I pray that out of his glorious riches he may strengthen you with power through his Spirit in your inner being, so that Christ may dwell in your hearts through faith. And I pray that you, being rooted and established in love, may have power, together with all the Lord's holy people, to grasp how wide and long and high and deep is the love of Christ, and to know this love that surpasses knowledge—that you may be filled to the measure of all the fullness of God. (Ephesians 3:14-19)

I am Everything You Need!

The Lord said I am everything you need. I am your food, your shelter, your job, your friend, your spouse, your protector, your guide, your counselor, your comforter, your strength! I am everything you need.

God said to Moses, "I am who I am. This is what you are to say to the Israelites: 'I am has sent me to you. (Exodus 3:14)

I have Got You

I've got you. That's the Lord's answer to my concern. Humbling but comforted to hear the preachers story that said, hold onto me, I've got you.

Come," he said. Then Peter got down out of the boat, walked on the water and came toward Jesus. But when he saw the wind, he was afraid and, beginning to sink, cried out, "Lord, save me!" Immediately Jesus reached out his hand and caught him. "You of little faith," he said, "why did you doubt?" (Matthew 14:29-3)

Life

Life is not simple, and God's ways are not our ways. Making the right decision may come at a cost. But in God's eternal plan, His blessings arrive in due time.

For the eyes of the Lord range throughout the earth to strengthen those whose hearts are fully committed to him. You have done a foolish thing, and from now on you will be at war. (2 Chronicles 16:9)

Love Your Neighbor

Love your neighbor. That's the greatest commandment. If we were all to do this, there would be less strife, murders, lying, cheating and even road rage. We would be more considerate of others, and that would be very impacting.

The ideal world indeed. Is it possible? Maybe not, but we can strive towards it, and with our Lord's supernatural help, we would get close.

The second is this: Love your neighbor as yourself. There is no commandment greater than these. (Mark 12:31)

The Lord--My GPS

The Lord is my guide and my counselor. The one I can trust for directions in my life.

But I trust in you, Lord; I say, "You are my God." (Psalm 31:14)

Healer

Come, let us return to the Lord. He has torn us to pieces, but he will heal us as He did with my sickness. He has injured us, but he will bind up our wounds as He did in the success of my surgery.

After two days he will revive us. On the third day He will restore us, that we may live in his presence. Let us acknowledge the Lord; let us press on to acknowledge him. As surely as the sun rises, He will appear; He will come to me like the winter rains, like the spring rains that water the earth. (Hosea 6:2)

The Journey Begins

The journey begins. The growth and development of my goal into life form. Holding the Lord my God's hand, I will follow His lead. My God is more than able. Help me Lord to keep the faith. Help me Lord to hold onto your unchanging hand.

I will instruct you and teach you in the way you should go. I will counsel you with my loving eye on you. (Psalm 32:8)

Life's Storms

When life feels like a storm-tossed sea with crashing waves of pain and grief, turn to the Lord and trust in Him, He'll give you peace and bring relief.

It's better to go through the storm with Christ than to have smooth sailing without Him.

Make Jesus your first option when the storms of life threaten you. Peace. Be Still. (Mark 4:35)

God's Reassurance

At the lowest point in my life, the Lord provides His comforting reassurance to lean on Him only. To trust Him to accomplish His purpose and plans for my life. He will cover the shortfall in my needs through His reassurance that He will not let the righteous perish nor his seed beg bread.

Lord give me the strength, the faith, the hope, the confidence, the complete trust and dependence needed today. Thank you, Lord, for answered prayers.

So, do not fear, for I am with you do not be dismayed, for I am your God. I will strengthen you and help you; I will uphold you with my righteous right hand. (Isaiah 41:10)

God Provides Even When Asleep

God provides for us even when we are asleep. Such a comforting assurance to know He is there. He knows. He keeps. He Provides. Fret not yourself, for it is useless for you to work from early morning until late at night just to get food to eat. God provides for those he loves even while they sleep.

In vain you rise early and stay up late, toiling for food to eat—for he grants sleep to those he loves. (Psalm 127:2)

Secret of Happiness

Augustine said that we get lost in loving ourselves but found in loving others. Expressed another way, the secret of happiness is not getting our face right but giving our hearts away, giving our lives away, giving ourselves away, in love.

Give thanks to the Lord, for he is good; his love endures forever. (Psalm 118:1)

When God Humbles

God will humble and test our resolutions to Him. This verse was profound as it stated clearly the purpose of my experience far away from home. It seems it brought me down to the lowest my life has ever experienced. The purpose was to humble me. To show me that I can live on Christ's merciful provisions for me. Thank you, Jesus. Thank you, Lord.

Remember how the Lord your God led you all the way in the wilderness these forty years, to humble and test you in order to know what was in your heart, whether or not you would keep his commands. He humbled you, causing you to hunger and then feeding you with manna, which neither you nor your ancestors had known, to teach you that man does not live on bread alone but on every word, that comes from the mouth of the LORD. Your clothes did not wear out and your feet did not swell during these forty years. Know then in your heart that as a man disciplines his son, so the LORD your God disciplines you. (Deuteronomy 8:25)

Go and you will be told what to do

When God says go, just Do it. Have Faith; He will Guide our every step if we stay focused. "Who are you, lord?" "I am Jesus, now get up and go ..., and you will be told what you must do."

Who are you, lord? Saul asked. And the voice replied, I am Jesus, the one you are persecuting! Now get up and go into the city, and you will be told what you must do (Acts 9:5-6)

God will Help

For I am the Lord, your God, who takes hold of your right hand and says to you, do not fear; I will help you.

So, do not fear for I am with you. Do not be dismayed, for I am your God. I will strengthen you and help you; I will uphold you with my righteous right hand. (Isaiah 41:10)

How Long

Lord, please hear my prayer as I call on you today.

How long Lord? I asked. But it's not for me to lose faith and question your ways. For your ways are better than mine. My ways want a quick fix, but your ways refine me like pure gold, pure genuine gold that will take me through the furnace.

Lord help me to bear your refinement, your training. Help me to wait patiently on you in confidence, remaining steadfast in the knowledge that you have done great things in the past, and you will do it again for me. Teach me to wait.

Thank you, Lord. Thanks for your strength. Thanks for your divine courage and most of all, your peace as often I don't understand. But I trust you.

Lord, hear my prayer. Listen to my cry for help. Pay attention to my sobbing. I'm like a guest in your home. I'm only a visitor, like all my family who lived before me. (Psalm 39:12)

First Humbled Then Blessed

Lord the revelation! First you humble then you Bless. Adam was banned—humbled. Then from him, all men descended.

Moses grew up with the rich, later ran away, humbled. Then blessed when he led the children of Israel out and was used by God to part the Red Sea.

Joseph was a slave who was molded in the house of the rich and powerful. He was later banished to prison. Then he was elevated to manage the nation's resources during the famine.

Paul, the persecutor, was humbled through blindness. Then he was blessed to become a chief evangelist, writer, and leader of all times. Help me Lord to remember to hold on for as you humble, then you bless.

Humble yourselves before the Lord, and he will lift you up. (James 4:10)

Out of the Ashes, I Rise!

Out of the Ashes, I rise stronger, ready to conquer! Lord, I thank you for the work you are doing in my life. After my exiled period of resistance and disobedience, I have learnt. Now please Lord help me to rebuild the needed areas of my life. As you did with the people of Babylon, also do with me. Out of the ashes, I rise—stronger. Because my help comes from the Lord! Thank you, Jesus. Thank you, Lord.

My help comes from the LORD, the Maker of heaven and earth. (Psalm 121:2)

God's Instructions

Woke up early, read for a while, then fell back asleep while praying. Woke up with a start to the words "just get up and go! Get up and go." Then I turned on the TV and heard preacher Dr. Charles Stanley emphasize the scripture verse; *I will be with you, I will not leave you.* You will have Success wherever you go because the Lord is with you. Then Dr. Stanley ended with the words "you can face any situation with Him, or without Him. So, choose wisely.

Been asking, pleading, and seeking God's guidance and direction with an issue that was bigger than me. Could the Lord be clearer in His response to my prayers?

Lord, please help me to always trust and obey you.

No one will be able to stand against you all the days of your life. As I was with Moses, so I will be with you; I will never leave you nor forsake you. (Joshua 1:5)

He's Intentional

Open my eyes Lord that I may see your will and your direction for my life. Let me not stray from you. Remove disappointment, doubt, and fears. Help me step forward in (God) confidence knowing that you're in control of my every move because you are intentional.

And Elisha prayed, "Open his eyes, Lord, so that he may see." Then the Lord opened the servant's eyes, and he looked and saw the hills full of horses and chariots of fire all around Elisha." 2 Kings 6:17

I Am What You Need

God is the Great I AM. I am what you need. I am your provider, protector, leader, guide, comforter, deliverer! I am what you need.

God said to Moses, I am who I am. This is what you are to say to the Israelites: 'I am has sent me to you. (Exodus 3:14)

Feeling Overwhelmed or Manipulated?

When feeling manipulators at work, remember God's words to not be afraid. Just leave everything up to Him.

So, do not fear, for I am with you; do not be dismayed, for I am your God. I will strengthen you and help you; I will uphold you with my righteous right hand. "All who rage against you will surely be ashamed and disgraced; those who oppose you will be as nothing and perish. Though you search for your enemies, you will not find them. Those who wage war against you will be as nothing at all. For I am the Lord your God who takes hold of your right hand and says to you, do not fear; I will help you. Do not be afraid, you worm Jacob, little Israel, do not fear, for I myself will help you," declares the Lord, your Redeemer, the Holy One of Israel. (Isaiah 41:10-14)

God's Love

I have always loved you, says the lord. It's always pleasing to hear your loved one say those words. But what is even more wonderful for me is the Lord's love for me even when I fail. His love holds firm. Today, I'm reminded to love Him as He first loved me.

I have always loved you," says the LORD. But you retort, "Really? How have you loved us?" And the LORD replies, "This is how I showed my love for you: I loved your ancestor Jacob," (Malachi 1:2)

Life

Life is not simple, and God's ways are not our ways. Making the right decision may come at a cost. But in God's eternal plan, His blessings arrive in due time.

*"For the eyes of the Lord range throughout the earth to strengthen those whose hearts are fully committed to him. You have done a foolish thing, and from now on you will be at war." – Chronicles **16:9***

God's Ways are Not Our Ways

When Peter decided to fight a war to save Jesus by cutting off the ear of one of the soldiers Jesus stopped him and told him to put away his sword. One would think that Peter was doing the right thing by defending his lord. But no, our Lord's way differs from ours. He always has a bigger plan. Lord, please make me wise to see your plan today, tomorrow and always.

"Jesus commanded Peter, "Put your sword away! Shall I not drink the cup the Father has given me?"(John 18:11)

God's Moments

Gods moments—experiencing Quiet Moments with God, calms my spirit and gives me peace.

I look behind me and you're there. Then up ahead and you're there too. Your reassuring presence coming and going. This is too much. Too wonderful. (Psalm 139:5)

Lord Help!

When life knocks you down, you're in the perfect position to pray (our daily bread). Lord, please help. Please intervene today. You know my needs, my wants my weaknesses, my fears. Lord, please have mercy on me today. Thank you for your strength and giving me the will and power to persist. I can only do it through you who give me the strength. In Jesus name, Amen.

"Let us then approach God's throne of grace with confidence, so that we may receive mercy and find grace to help us in our time of need." – (Hebrews 4:16)

The Moment God Speaks

The moment God speaks is the time he wants you to respond. The moment God speaks is His timing. Do not assume that you are not ready or equipped. Who God calls, he equips just like David with Goliath; Abraham with his son; Esther, Joseph, Paul, Moses, and many others.

So even when I am afraid it will not stop me. I will respond to your call. I will walk in God-confidence knowing he leads, guides, directs, and grants me favor along the way.

Now may the God of peace..., equip you with everything good for doing his will, and may he work in us what is pleasing to him, through Jesus Christ, to whom be glory for ever and ever. (Hebrews 13:20-21)

Hope

This week the lord has placed the word Hope in my heart. When we have hope, we can go on. Let me rephrase—because we have Hope we can go on. God remains in charge of us. In faith, we can go on because we trust Him.

Trust in the Lord with all your heart, (Proverbs 3:5)

Inside of Me

I was thinking about the Lord and what He means to me. So, I created a replica of God inside, and around me. He is at the center of everything. I just want Him to work through me. Nothing else matters unless He is working in our plans. Let's keep praying and trusting. In peace, know that He will work things out for us.

To them God has chosen to make known among the Gentiles the glorious riches of this mystery, which is Christ in you, the hope of glory. (Colossians 1:27)

I Jumped!

Inspired by Ruth, an 80-year-old at church, I jumped. God protected me as He did to her as she skydived and showed that indeed we can do all things through Christ. Thank you, Lord, for your protection and using this experience as the tool of encouragement to always be courageous in pursuing our dreams with Christ at the head.

If any of you lacks wisdom, you should ask God, who gives generously to all without finding fault, and it will be given to you. But when you ask, you must believe and not doubt, because the one who doubts is like a wave of the sea, blown and tossed by the wind. (James 1:5-6)

Fear But Faith

You are not alone I did a tandem jump 14,000 ft.! As I was asked to jump from the little plane, I was scared as ever! But I did it because I was strapped to a guide. So, though I was terrified, the assurance that the guide was there to pull out the parachute when the time came gave me confidence in the midst of my Fear. In the midst of our fall, the guide pulled, and we floated in mid-air enjoying the beauty of nature's ambience below. I was confident because I had support.

Lord may I bask in the assurance that you are there with me. In the midst of life's pain, you've got me. My landing will be safe cause you have got me. Thank you, Jesus. Thank you, Lord.

Do not be afraid, for I am with you (Isaiah 43:5)

God Makes a Way

When God makes a way for us, that way usually take time. But a word of comfort at that time allows God's healing ingredients to be applied to our situation.

Teach me your way, Lord; lead me in a straight path because of my oppressors. (Psalm 27:11)

When Mistakes Maim

Lord, as my 18-year-old college student starts making her decisions independently without the help of her mom, please don't let her mistakes maim. Though some may leave scars, let them not maim or disable.

Forget the former things; do not dwell on the past. See, I am doing a new thing. Now it springs up; do you not perceive it? I am making a way in the wilderness and streams in the wasteland. (Isaiah 43:18-19)

Memorialize

When God steps in He does things that will work in your memory. Yes, He does. Just like the woman with the perfume, she did a seemingly very simple thing that turned out so profound. Her action has lasted centuries.

Lord when you plant your work in my heart, please help me to follow you. Help me to listen to your leading. Father, please help me to work as unto you, and not for anything else. Thank you, Jesus. Thank you, Lord.

Truly I tell you, wherever this gospel is preached throughout the world, what she has done will also be told, in memory of her. (Matthew 26:13)

Our Nation

Lord, we Praise you for your blessing and we cry for your intervention in the affairs of our lives and that of our nations worldwide.

I urge, then, first of all, that petitions, prayers, intercession and thanksgiving be made for all people –"- (1Timothy 2:1)

New Attitude

It's funny how the apostles Paul and Barnabas obeyed God, shook the dust off their feet, and went on their way rejoicing. This attitude is important in times of change when we meet objections to God-given instructions when others don't understand.

Ignore the naysayers and obey. Simply obey the Lord. Devote yourself to Him, and He will take care of your future. Move on from the red light. He has given you the green. Trust Him and move on in spite of objections. Once we trust God and devote our way to him, He will give us his joy and peace for the future.

If anyone will not welcome you or listen to your words, leave that home or town and shake the dust off your feet. (Matthew 10:14)

Rejoice

When we have done all we can do, we can let go and let God. Then we go on our way rejoicing.

Rejoice in the Lord always. Again, I say rejoice. (Philippians 4:4)

It's Never Too Late

It's never too late to become who you might have been.

As Jesus approached Jericho, a blind man was sitting by the roadside begging. 36 When he heard the crowd going by, he asked what was happening. They told him, "Jesus of Nazareth is passing by." He called out, "Jesus, Son of David, have mercy on me!" Those who led the way rebuked him and told him to be quiet, but he shouted all the more, "Son of David, have mercy on me!" Jesus stopped and ordered the man to be brought to him. When he came near, Jesus asked him, "What do you want me to do for you?" "Lord, I want to see," he replied. Jesus said to him, "Receive your sight; your faith has healed you." (Luke 18:35-43)

Nice to Finally Meet You

New or recommitted believer prays, Dear God, nice to finally meet you. Thank you for all the blessings you have bestowed on me.

Therefore, if anyone is in Christ, the new creation has come. The old has gone, the new is here! (2 Corinthians 5:17)

God of the Impossible

My Lord is the God of the impossible.

You are my God, and I will give thanks; you are my God, and I will exalt you. (Psalm 118:28 NIVUK)

Miracles

A miracle is defined as "something so difficult only God can do it." Therefore, as many examples recorded; Abraham had Isaac at 100 years old; the Lord delivered his people from exile; a virgin gave birth to a savior.

So, do not worry. The Lord is working things out for you according to His will. Simply trust, have faith, and continue to believe. It will come through soon because nothing is too hard for the Lord.

The Lord said to Abraham "is anything too hard for The Lord?" (Genesis 18:14.)

Negatives...But Not in God's Sight

Sometimes we have what society perceives as negatives—be it gender, age, ethnicity, financial acumen, status, education, and more. But society's negatives are God's positives. He sees, he cares, and He will come through using the same society to bless us as He did with Moses when he was pulled from the river as a baby. He was safe right there in Pharaoh's house.

Oh, what a sense of humor our dear Lord has!

For we are God's handiwork, created in Christ Jesus to do good works, which God prepared in advance for us to do. (Ephesians 2:10)

Go Back to The Basics First

The Lord said, go back to the basics first. Understand the value of getting what you need, and pass by what you want—some nice to have things and some totally unnecessary things. Then I the Lord will bless you later. Hold on and learn what He is taking you through now.

Joshua told the people, "Consecrate yourselves, for tomorrow the Lord will do amazing things among you. (Joshua 3:5)

I Have Always Loved You

I have always loved you ...says the lord. It's always pleasing to hear your loved one say those words. But what is wonderful is the Lord's love for me even when I fail. His love holds firm. Today I am reminded to love Him as He loved me

I have always loved you," says the LORD. But you retort, "Really? How have you loved us?" And the LORD replies, "This is how I showed my love for you: I loved your ancestor Jacob," (Malachi 1:2)

Friday the 13th

Banish negativity. Welcome, the Jesus problem solver. You are the great I am. The Great I Am is Lord over Friday the 13th. Face the day with the sword of the spirit. There is never a day when we don't need to pray

So, I will come to put you on trial. I will be quick to testify against sorcerers, adulterers and perjurers, against those who defraud laborers of their wages, who oppress the widows and the fatherless, and deprive the foreigners among you of justice, but do not fear me," says the Lord Almighty. (Malachi 3:5)

Overwhelmed

In the midst of life's challenges and disappointments, we get sad and feel defeated. In our own minds, we see life as overwhelming. But that only happens when we forget how the Lord works for us. Our God surrounds us with His mighty hand and His mighty power. With Him on our side, we can move any mountain. With Him on our side, there is no fear. He protects, guards and covers.

"Don't be afraid," the prophet answered. "Those who are with us are more than those who are with them." Elisha prayed, "Lord, open my servant's eyes so he can see." Then the Lord opened his eyes. He looked up and saw the hills. He saw that Elisha was surrounded by horses and chariots. Fire was all around them." (2 Kings 6:16-17)

Open My Eyes Lord

Open my eyes Lord that I may see your will, your direction for my life. Let me not stray from you. Remove disappointment doubt and fears. Help me step forward in God-confidence knowing that you are in control of my every move and you are intentional.

"And Elisha prayed, "Open his eyes, Lord, so that he may see." Then the Lord opened the servant's eyes, and he looked and saw the hills full of horses and chariots of fire all around Elisha." (2 Kings 6:17)

Open the Flood Gates

Lord open the floodgates of heaven and let your favor reign on me. Lord I receive your many, many blessings in Jesus name.

Bring the whole tithe into the storehouse, that there may be food in my house. Test me in this," says the Lord Almighty, "and see if I will not throw open the floodgates of heaven and pour out so much blessing that there will not be room enough to store it. (Malachi3:10)

Press On

Persevere. Endure hardships as a good soldier of Christ. Press on. Hold on. Never Give Up.

I press on toward the goal to win the prize for which God has called me heavenward in Christ Jesus. (Philippians 3:14)

Be still. Be Patient. Wait.

When everything's coming your way, you are probably in the wrong lane. Are you on the path where it seems nothing—no job, money, church family or more is coming your way. Lord, does that mean we are not in your will?

Strange, sad, alone? Relocating to a different area does come with the challenge and excitement to start anew even when you are afraid. But then we trust you. Lord teach us to wait. Give us the patience to trust only you. Because you are the one true, kind, wise, and all-knowing God. Lord help us to trust you.

Be still. Be patient. Wait for the Lord to act. Don't be upset when other people succeed. Don't be upset when they carry out their evil plans. (Psalm 37:7)

Prepare

Lord help me to be more like a squirrel scurrying, planning and preparing for the future. Help me to be less like a deer—meaning less reactive, less of taking whatever comes my way. Though both animals are important, and you take care of both.

With this, I know that I can do all things through Christ who gives me the strength. Thank you, Lord, for taking my hand and leading me along the right path, though rocky it may be at times. Lead me to the light at the end of the tunnel.

Trust in the Lord with all your heart and lean not on your own understanding. In all your ways acknowledge Him and He will direct your path. (Pro 3:5-6)

Only God

Trust in the Lord even when you don't understand. In everything let Him know. Seek His will, and He will work things out. A family member lost her job just days after agreeing to host other family members going through a tough financial situation. In the midst of this decision, this tragic circumstance unfolded. But God came through.

So always acknowledge Him. Tell Him all your needs, hurts, pain, and your heart's desires. He will work things out according to his will and purpose for your life.

When the cares of my heart are many, your consolations cheer my soul. (Psalm 94:19)

Praise Him

Praise the Lord for His dramatic answers! All I can do is just shout with friends and family. Praise Him for faith and answered prayers.

Praise Him. Praise Him in the morning. Praise Him in the noontime. Thank you, Jesus, for your sure answer to prayers. Love you lord. Bless you, lord.

Bless the LORD, O my soul, and all that is within me, bless His holy name. (Psalm 103:1)

Plenty More Than Enough

Then you will have more than plenty. Lord help me to wait for your perfect timing.

"Then the Lord will send rain on your land at the right time. He'll send rain in the fall and in the spring. You will be able to gather your grain. You will also be able to make olive oil and fresh wine." (Deuteronomy 11:14)

Quiet Rest

Find a Quiet place and rest. You will be of more use to others.

"Then Jesus said, "Let's go off by ourselves to a quiet place and rest awhile." He said this because there were so many people coming and going that Jesus and his apostles didn't even have time to eat. So, they left by boat for a quiet place, where they could be alone." (Mark 6:31-32)

The Path is Ready

You have seen for yourself what the Lord has already done for you. So, do not be afraid. He will provide that answer to your prayers. So, get ready because you soon will not have the time to do all the things you now have the time to do.

Increase our faith, Lord. Make us over. Build our confidence. Make us bold. Please hold our hands firmly and take us along the path that you have created. The path that you have prepared. The path that is now ready and to which we are scared to go alone. We give you thanks and praise you, Lord.

Great is the Lord, and highly to be praised, And His greatness is unsearchable. (Psalm 145:3)

Pulled Back to Push forward

Sometimes God pulls us back to push us forward. Lord give me the strength to hold on when you decide to pull me back in order to propel me ahead. I look to you, I wait on you patiently, sometimes impatiently. But still, I wait in faith.

This is the confidence we have in approaching God: that if we ask anything according to his will, he hears us. And if we know that he hears us - whatever we ask - we know that we have what we asked of him. (1 John 5:14-15).

Peace

Lord grant me the serenity to accept the things I cannot change, the courage to change the things I can, and the wisdom to know the difference.

Cast your cares on the LORD and he will sustain you; he will never let the righteous be shaken. (Psalm 55:22)

Perseverance

Do not grow weary in doing good. Do not give up. If the Lord is using a seemingly insurmountable challenge to produce perseverance in your life, do not give up. Let Him produce in you, character and through character hope. When trials intrude to slow down your life it would be easy for you to give in. But through perseverance, you will overcome strife. So just keep on plodding, because with Christ you can win.

Let us not become weary in doing good, for at the proper time we will reap a harvest if we do not give up. (Galatians 6:9)

Take Your Position

Listen, this is what The Lord says, "do not be afraid." Do not be discouraged by your mighty army of personal needs. For the battle is not yours, but the Lord's. Tomorrow, step out despite your needs. Just step out. You will not even need to fight. Just take your position, then stand still and watch the Lord's victory. He is with you.

Oh you, don't be afraid or discouraged. Go out despite your needs. For the Lord is with you. Learn from the people of old. They had faith. They had trust. They had hope! Once the Lord spoke to them, they just did what He said. They stepped forward in faith while praising Him!

I found that many times it was their practice to praise God even before they experienced His answer. People like David; Solomon, when he was about to build the temple; Moses; King Jehoshaphat during his early Reign. These individuals included praise as a part of their plans before they experienced victory.

Oh Lord! Please help me to be like them. To praise you in the midst of my troubles. To praise you even when I can't see my way.

Help me to praise you, Lord. Increase my praise. Increase my trust. Help me to praise you before I receive your answer. Then help me to praise you after I receive the victory. Take me to the valley of blessing. Take me to the valley of praise. Grant me protection on every side! Lord, I love you. Lord, I praise you because when I'm weak, then I am strong. Praises.

He said: "Listen, King Jehoshaphat and all who live in Judah and Jerusalem! This is what the Lord says to you: 'Do not be afraid or discouraged because of this vast army. For the battle is not yours, but God's. Tomorrow march down against them. They will be climbing up by the Pass of Ziz, and you will find them at the end of the gorge in the Desert of Jeruel. You will not have to fight this battle. Take up your positions; stand firm and see the deliverance the Lord will give you, Judah and Jerusalem. Do not be afraid; do not be discouraged. Go out to face them tomorrow, and the Lord will be with you." (2 Chronicles 20:15-17)

Prayer

Prayer imparts the power to walk and not faint.
—Chambers

He gives strength to the weary and increases the power of the weak. Even youths grow tired and weary, and young men stumble and fall; but those who hope in the Lord will renew their strength. They will soar on wings like eagles; they will run and not grow weary, they will walk and not be faint. (Isaiah 40:29-31)

Our Reaction When God Answers Prayers

Did you know that sometimes the very things we ask the Lord for are the very things that (when He grants them) affect our relationship with Him? We plead for a job, family, money, marriage, children, and more. Yet, when He grants our wish, we become too busy to spend time with Him; to read His word, and to worship Him at church. No wonder He sometimes takes a while to answer our prayers—because He knows our future.

Lord, thank you for your grace and forgiveness. Help me to make the time to always remain close to you.

Blessed is the man who makes the Lord his trust, who does not turn to the proud, to those who go astray after a lie! (Psalm 40:4)

Jesus Prayed the Same Prayer Again

Jesus prayed the same prayer again. It struck me, if He did that, then so should we. Pray once. Pray twice, thrice, or more. Let's bring our cares to Him. He will hear. He will answer in His time.

Jesus prayed the same prayer again (Mark 14:39)

Panic or Pray?

Prayer always works. God's supernatural power is ever present, comforting, and just calming. Thank God for His assurance, and presence in our times of need.

In my distress, anxiety, and fear, Lord teach me to rely on you and draw close to you. Then I know I will be able to stand strong in your power and won't be dependent on my own strength.

Then Asa called to the Lord his God and said, "Lord, there is no one like you to help the powerless against the mighty. Help us, Lord our God, for we rely on you, and in your name we have come against this vast army. Lord, you are our God; do not let mere mortals prevail against you." (2 Chronicles 14:11)

Pray Like It's Up to God: Act Like It's Up to You

Pray like it's up to God; act like it's up to you. Over, and over again, God has told us to take our problems and anxieties to Him. Not to worry about anything but to pray about everything. Tell God what you need and thank Him for all He has done.

But once you have finished praying for your problems, don't expect angels to finish building your walls. Pick up your trowel and finish the job God has given you. Work hard for God is working in you. I once read that too many people pray like little children who knock on doors then run away. Oh, that we would stay the course in faith.

Jabez cried out to the God of Israel, "Oh, that you would bless me and enlarge my territory! Let your hand be with me, and keep me from harm so that I will be free from pain." And God granted his request. (1 Chronicles 4:10)

And It Came to Pass

And it came to pass. Nothing remains. This verse reminds us that everything passes through. Nothing remains at a standstill. It is all just passing through.

Lord, please hold my friend's hand, quiet her heart, and give her comfort, peace, and love as she passes through this difficult time.

When you pass through the waters, I will be with you; and when you pass through the rivers, they will not sweep over you. When you walk through the fire, you will not be burned; the flames will not set you ablaze. (Isaiah 43:2)

What He Said He Will Do

Be confident. What the Lord has said, He will do. Trust him today.

"From the east I summon a bird of prey; from a far-off land, a man to fulfill my purpose. What I have said, that I will bring about; what I have planned, that I will do." (Isaiah 46:11)

Answer Me

I'm listening, answer me Lord...please.

"Answer me quickly, Lord; my spirit fails. Do not hide your face from me or I will be like those who go down to the pit. Let the morning bring me word of your unfailing love, for I have put my trust in you. Show me the way I should go, for to you I entrust my life." (Psalm 143:7-8)

And it Came to Pass

Nothing remains. Just realized in this verse that everything is about Passing through. It will not remain. It's just passing through. Lord, please hold my friend's hand, quiet her Heart, and give her lots of comfort, Peace, and love as she passes through this difficult time. Thank you, Jesus, thank you, lord.

When you pass through the waters, I will be with you; and when you pass through the rivers, they will not sweep over you. When you walk through the fire, you will not be burned; the flames will not set you ablaze. – (Isaiah 43:2)

The Lord Will Provide

So, though you are in grave need, be confident and know that the Lord will provide for all your needs according to His riches in glory (and by the way, He is wealthy).

Abraham called that place the Lord will provide. (Genesis 22:14)

God Has a Purpose

In everything, there is God's purpose. Look for God's Purpose.

From the east I summon a bird of prey; from a far-off land, a man to fulfill my purpose. What I have said, that I will bring about; what I have planned, that I will do. (Isaiah 46:11)

Like Daniel, This Is My Prayer

Oh, our God, hear your servant's prayer. Listen as I plead. For your own sake, Lord, smile again on (me) your desolate sanctuary. Oh my God, lean down and listen to me. Open your eyes and see my despair. See how your child that bears your name—lies in ruins. We make this plea, not because we deserve help, but because of your mercy.

O Lord, hear. O Lord, forgive. O Lord, listen and act! For your own sake, do not delay, O my God, for your people and your city bear your name. (Daniel 9:17-19)

Pray

There is never a day when we don't need to pray. Banish negativity. Welcome Jesus problem solver. You're the great I am. The great I am—is Lord over everything that distracts. Let's face the day with the sword of the spirit!

I can do all Things through Christ. (Philippians 4:13)

Rebuild

Lord I thank you for the work you're doing in my life. After my exiled period of pride, resistance, then obedience and learning, please help me rebuild. As you did with the people of Babylon, also do with me. Out of the ashes, I rise—stronger because my help comes from the Lord.

My help cometh from the Lord, which made heaven and earth. (Psalm 121:2)

Testify

He said it, publish His glorious deeds among the nation. Tell others what the Lord has done for you. This is his direction. Praise Him. Great is the Lord. He is worthy of praise.

Publish his glorious deeds among the nations. Tell everyone about the amazing things he does. (1 Chronicles 16:24)

Shaken Together and Running Over

Remember the more positives we do, the Lord replenishes. He gives back to us pressed down, shaken together, and running over.

Give, and it shall be given unto you; good measure, pressed down, and shaken together, and running over, shall men give into your bosom. For with the same measure that ye mete withal it shall be measured to you again. (Luke 6:38)

God's Word Quenches

Various metaphors are used in Scripture to describe God's Word: a mirror (James 1:23); fire and a hammer (Jer. 23:29), a lamp (Ps. 119:105), water (Eph. 5:26), a two-edged sword (Heb. 4:12), a seed (1 Peter 1:23), food (Job 23:12), and milk (1 Peter 2:2). The Word of God reveals, consumes, breaks, illuminates, purifies, convicts, regenerates, satisfies, and nourishes the believer. It is not enough to know God's Word; we need to obey it. ~David MaCasland

Do not merely listen to the word, and so deceive yourselves. Do what it says. Anyone who listens to the word but does not do what it says is like someone who looks at his face in a mirror and, after looking at himself, goes away and immediately forgets what he looks like. But whoever looks intently into the perfect law that gives freedom, and continues in it—not forgetting what they have heard, but doing it—they will be blessed in what they do. (James 1:22-25)

Rock of Ages

Rock of Ages cleft for me, let me hide myself in thee.

Trust in the Lord forever, for the Lord is a Rock of ages (Isiah 26:4)

Enough for Each Day

Do not worry God always provides. Learn to trust God for your daily needs.

He provided manna for the Israelites when they were in the desert. He fed 5000 people when they were away without food using a little boy's small serving of fish, and even had leftovers. He provided for the woman with the little bit of flour and olive oil when she told the prophet, Elijah, that she was going to eat her last meal and die. He used the ravens to feed Elijah when he was in the deserted place. Elijah was tired, hungry and depressed. The Lord came through using what seemed impossible, creatures of the earth—a raven, to meet Elijah's needs.

So be confident. Tell the Lord your needs then trust him. He will provide your daily provisions if we lean on him daily. He's got us. He will provide for us day by day, as we need it.

Then the word of the Lord came to Elijah: "Leave here, turn eastward and hide in the Kerith Ravine, east of the Jordan. You will drink from the brook, and I have directed the ravens to supply you with food there (1 Kings 17:2-4)

Quiet Rest

It's important to rest. Our Lord instructed us to get away for quiet peace and rest. It calms our soul.

Then, because so many people were coming and going that they did not even have a chance to eat, he said to them, "Come with me by yourselves to a quiet place and get some rest." (Mark 6:31)

Dwindling Resources

God at times allows our resources to dwindle so that He can accomplish His purposes in our life. It's when we are weak that He is made strong.

So, do not fear, for I am with you; do not be dismayed, for I am your God. I will strengthen you and help you; I will uphold you with my righteous right hand." (Isaiah 41:10)

When the Alarm Goes Off

Ever notice that when the alarm goes off, that's when we are pulling the covers to get the nicest sleep? But to ignore, need I say more? Let's ensure that we are ready when the Lord's alarm goes off—for a project he instructed us to do; or for his return. To ignore, need I say more?

So, you also must be ready, because the Son of Man will come at an hour when you do not expect him. (Mathew 24:44)

Enemies and Manipulators

Help me Jesus, help me, Lord. Fight for me. Bring shame to those who manipulate. Rebuild my confidence and trust to remember that you have done great things and you remain in charge. Just like you did for David with Saul; and Hezekiah with Naaman.

O Lord, oppose those who oppose me. Fight those who fight against me. Help me to put on your armor and take up your shield. Prepare for battle, and come to my aid. Lift up your spear and javelin against those who pursue me. Let me hear you say, "I will give you victory!"

Bring shame and disgrace on those trying to kill me. Turn them back and humiliate those who want to harm me. Blow them away like chaff in the wind— a wind sent by the angel of the Lord. Make their path dark and slippery, with the angel of the Lord pursuing them.

They repay me evil for good. I am sick with despair. (Psalms 35:12)

God's Refining

At bible study, the topic was about Shadrach, Meshach and Abednego, and the fire. The takeaway for me was how, at times, the Lord takes us through some things to renew us, and He also takes us through some things to refine us. I believe He is refining me at this point in my life. I pray that I will be patient.

Then those who feared the Lord talked with each other, and the Lord listened and heard. A scroll of remembrance was written in his presence concerning those who feared the Lord and honored his name. (Malachi 3:16)

Blessings for The Righteous

God will deal with our enemies and care for us. Let us always be in tune with a continuous spirit of prayer ...the Lord will bless us.

Surely, Lord, you bless the righteous; you surround them with your favor as with a shield. (Psalm 5:12)

The Lord Rescues

You come to me with spears, swords, and javelins but I come to you in the name of the Lord, for the battle is His. The Lord is with you; therefore, you will succeed at everything you do. Just trust him even when things don't make sense. He'll take care of you just like He did with David.

The Lord is close to the brokenhearted; he rescues those whose spirits are crushed. (Psalm 34:18)

He Remains in Control

At the hospital, Janine's 85-year-old dad bid his last goodbye to his adult children. He had lived a good life and was ready to go. Always in control, he gave them instructions as to what to do, where to go, and what to say as they made his final arrangements. He then told his girls to leave the hospital and go home. He encouraged them that all will be well. He was confident that the night would be his last because he was in control.

As morning alighted, her dad opened his eyes in sharp amazement. He was still 'here.' Though he was ready and willing to go, the quietness of his planned passing refuted his well-made plans. He was disappointed.

What Janine's dad tried to do was to make plans. But our Lord remains in control of every single aspect of our lives. He decides when we are born, and when he will call us home. There is nothing we can do about it until *He is ready*.

May you always be willing to follow his plan.

A man's heart plans his way, but the Lord directs his steps. (Proverbs 16:9)

Scared to Fail. Scared to Succeed

Lord, sometimes I'm scared. Scared of failure; scared of success. But scare, or even fear has never stopped me. If anything, it fuels me to achieve.

Success puts me in the spotlight, and I'm not sure if I can handle the spotlight. Can you please take over? I had this idea ...you must have put in my heart. I followed through, and it's done. Now I'm feeling afraid.

But as always, I'll find comfort in knowing that all things work together for good to those who love the Lord. Those who are called according to His purpose. Lord, I know that when I'm afraid I can trust in you. In all my ways I will acknowledge you, Lord, to direct my path.

Today, I acknowledge you, Lord. Take over. Work supernaturally, in your way and in your time. Thank you, Jesus. Thank you, Lord.

And we know that all things work together for good to them that love God, to them who are the called according to his purpose. (Romans 8:28)

Speak Out

When prompted by the Holy Spirit, don't be afraid. Speak out. He will give speech through you as He did Moses and Aaron.

One night the Lord spoke to Paul in a vision and told him, don't be afraid. Speak out. Don't be silent! (Acts 18:9)

Be Strong

The Lord's eyes roam to seek those who need Strength. Contrast with the devil who goes around seeking those he may devour. Choose to be strong in the Lord today. He will give you the Strength to overcome the storm you are facing in your life right now. Hold on tight. He's got you!

For the eyes of the Lord range throughout the earth to strengthen those whose hearts are fully committed to him. You have done a foolish thing, and from now on you will be at war. – (2 Chronicles 16:9)

Stand. Wait. Listen

After you've prayed, just stand. Wait and listen for God's replies. He's got your back.

Then those who feared the Lord talked with each other, and the Lord listened and heard. A scroll of remembrance was written in his presence concerning those who feared the Lord and honored his name. (Malachi 3:16)

Strong Enough

I was just thinking about the song *'Strong Enough.'* It came to mind because I'm weak. Though I know my job very well, the challenges around sometimes make it hard to do a great job. It was then that I remembered that I don't have to be 'strong' ...because God is strong enough for both of us.

May this remind you today that no matter how much we know in a new job/career, entrepreneurship endeavor, new life venture, sickness, or other circumstances, when the going gets rough, we can do all things through Christ.

I can do all this through him who gives me strength. (Philippians 4:13)

Pray Specifically

Let your prayers be specific. Just like Esther going before the king. Pray so that when the Lord answers your prayer you know, He did. The story of a Midwestern town that prayed for rain. The clergy and townspeople gathered for prayer, but only one little girl carried her umbrella. Carry your umbrella. Know that the Lord—He is our God and He answers prayers! Often even more than we could ask or think.

This is the confidence we have in approaching God: that if we ask anything according to his will, he hears us. And if we know that he hears us—whatever we ask—we know that we have what we asked of him. (1 John 5:14-15)

Stuck

If you're stuck and you can't see your way through, just hold on. God is leading you. God is coming through.

Forget the former things; do not dwell on the past. See, I am doing a new thing! Now it springs up; do you not perceive it? I am making a way in the wilderness and streams in the wasteland. (Isaiah 43:18-19).

Success

Success is closest when discouragement is at its greatest. Let go and let God. He will grant you success in all you do according to His will.

Oh Lord, save us; Oh Lord, grant us success. (Psalm 118:25)
At that time, I will gather you together. And I will bring you home I will give you honor and praise among all the nations on earth. I will bless you with great success again, says the Lord (Zephaniah 3:20).

Seek the Lord

If we seek the Lord, He will give us success.

O Lord, let your ear be attentive to the prayer of this your servant and to the prayer of your servants who delight in revering your name. Give your servant success today by granting him favor in the presence of this man (Nehemiah 1:11)

Stop

Stop. Take time out and refuel your soul.

Be still and know that I am God (Psalm 46:10)

Right on Time

Yeah, right on time. That's my God, He is always right on time. My daughter sent me a text that said, "Right on time". She was talking about the bus arrival for school.

But to me, it was one of our Lord's reassuring answers of His promise to meet our needs, desires, and goals in life. He is always right on time. Let's always trust Him. Before you call, God answers. Believe. He is ahead of us.

Before they call I will answer; while they are still speaking I will hear. (Isaiah 65:24)

The second Touch

Lord touch me again. Sprinkle me and give me that second touch. Today I believe. Today I receive your encouragement. My Shift is coming. Lord give me that second touch. Bring the right people; the right opportunities; the strength; the stamina, courage, and spirit of boldness. Thank you, Lord for the shift. Thank you for helping me to hold on. Help me to do the things that I could never do on my own and to be ready to receive your blessings today.

Joshua told the people, consecrate yourselves, for tomorrow the Lord will do amazing things among you. (Joshua 3:5)

In Sickness and In Pain

Father in heaven you know all things. You're the healer, protector, guide, and deliverer. I ask that you step in right now to heal and comfort the sick right now. Do your thing, Lord. Do your thing through the medical practitioners. Ease any pain Lord, ease. Grant your Peace. Thank you, Jesus. Thank you, Lord.

Trust in the Lord with all your heart and lean not on your own understanding;" (Proverbs 3:5)

Stand Still

Waiting to see what the Lord will do with your situation? Hold on. Keep on waiting. Stand still. Pray, consult the Lord. Listen for His reply.

Then move forward. The Lord will take care of the person or the situation and his/her army. Just like He did with Moses and the Israelites. When everything seemed hopeless, and they would perish—He parted the Red Sea, and they walked through on dry land. What a miracle. Just move forward, and the Lord will give you success.

Moses answered the people, "Do not be afraid. Stand firm and you will see the deliverance the Lord will bring you today. The Egyptians you see today you will never see again. (Exodus 14:13)

Strength - Plugin

The Creator of the universe knows no power failure. So, when we find ourselves weary and distressed, we need to plug into the true source of strength and life. We are more than conquerors through Him who loved us. The Christ who dwells within us is the greatest power we know. —Carmichael

He gives strength to the weary and increases the power of the weak. (Isaiah 40:29)

Suicide

Gethsemane. Could Jesus have committed suicide before going to the cross? Could he have backed out? Jesus saw what was going to happen to him. He knew. He could have backed out, run away, or even committed the unfathomable suicide. After all, He was going to die anyway, and the death on the cross was worse than any other—with its shame, disdain, and humiliation. But He didn't.

Thank you, Jesus, for staying the course. Thank you for not giving up. Because of your love and your grace, we can inherit eternal life. Father, when we are depressed, give us the strength to stay the course like Jesus did.

He went away a second time and prayed, my Father, if it is not possible for this cup to be taken away unless I drink it, may your will be done. (Matthew 26:42).

God's Definition of Success

Biblical definition of Success. Read the bible and do everything in it.

Never stop reading the Law (bible). Day and night, you must think about what it says. Make sure you do everything that is written in it. Then things will go well with you and you will have great success (Joshua 1:8).

Sometimes Strategies, Sometimes Miracles

David talked to The Lord, and he gave him two victories. One the Lord won supernaturally; the second he gave David strategies to win.

The people approached Jeremiah and asked him to pray for them. He prayed, and the Lord answered 10 days later.

Then there was Lazarus. Mary and Marta sent for The Lord. But He delayed and worked a huge miracle. He did that when Lazarus died but later was raised from the dead.

The Lord always seems to take long when there's a big victory around the corner. People are waiting for the Lord's answer. Teach us to wait Lord. Please teach us to wait.

May the favor of the Lord our God rest on us; May the Lord our God show us his favor. Lord, make what we do succeed. Please make what we do succeed. (Psalm 90:17 NIRV)

God is My Supplier

God supplies all my needs, so I will always have more than enough.

"From the east I summon a bird of prey; from a far-off land, a man to fulfill my purpose. What I have said, that I will bring about; what I have planned, that I will do." (Isaiah 46:12)

Mold Me and Make Me

Lord, please shape me according to your liking. According to your word. To accomplish your best. According to your will.

So, I went down to the potter's house, and I saw him working at the wheel. But the pot he was shaping from the clay was marred in his hands. So, the potter formed it into another pot, shaping it as seemed best to him. (Jeremiah 18:3-4)

Speak to my Heart

God, speak to my heart today. Lord help me to be quiet, so I may hear. So that I can listen.

Let the wise listen and add to their learning, and let the discerning get guidance. (Proverbs 1:5)

The Eyes of the Lord

The eyes of the Lord roam to seek those who need Strength. Contrast this with the devil that goes around seeking those he may devour. Choose to be strong in the Lord today. He will give you the strength to overcome the storm you are facing in your life right now. Hold on tight. He's got you.

"For the eyes of the Lord range throughout the earth to strengthen those whose hearts are fully committed to him. You have done a foolish thing, and from now on you will be at war." – (2 Chronicles 16:9)

When Experiencing Stress, Do Not Fear

Lord, I'm tired. Lord, I'm scared. Lord, I'm weak. Please help me because you said when I am weak, you are strong. Lord, I just want to go under the bed, curl up and hide until the problems go away. Please help me, Lord.

The rain is falling outside. It seems to be crying out for me. I feel so weak, so all alone. I feel like there is no one who I can talk with. I feel like David when Saul was pursuing him to take his life—for nothing—for doing good, for his loyalty and commitment.

Lord, I cry out to you. But I am confident that I have you, Lord, just like David had you. And for that reason, I want to remain in your loving arms, with the assurance that all of my help comes from you.

Today, as I enter the battlefield—even when I do not know why I am fighting, I commit my way to you. I cannot do it alone. You must take it over, take over the reign Lord, please take over the reign. Carry me. Lift me over this hurdle. Take away this problem, but if you can't (just yet), then do it for me. Let me hide myself in you.

Grant me peace, solace, and comfort. Help me trust that you will take over and all will be well in time. Today I look for an encouraging word from you to hold onto. Rebuild my confidence. Replace my doubts and fears with a sense of calm. Today I will stand still. Today, I will wait to see your miraculous intervention.

The time for me to set you free is near. I will soon save you. My powerful arm will make everything right among the nations. The islands will put their hope in me. They will wait for my powerful arm to act. (Isaiah 51:5)

Train Up a Child

I was comforted by Sisters' Bible Study President on the topic Breathe. The word spoke specifically to me when she said train up a child in the way he should go, and when he is old, he will not depart from it.

I have always been concerned about my youngest being away at college and not being able to attend church regularly. But this discussion comforted me that I did my part, and I am now to leave the rest to God. I will obey and trust Him knowing that all will be well because He remains in charge of my children.

Consider Abraham. He is the father of your people. Think about Sarah. She is your mother. When I chose Abraham, he did not have any children. But I blessed him and gave him many of them. You can be sure that I will comfort Zion's people. I will look with loving concern on all of their destroyed buildings. I will make their deserts like Eden. I will make their dry and empty land like my very own garden. Joy and gladness will be there. People will sing and give thanks to me. "Listen to me, my people. Pay attention, my nation. My law will go out to the nations. I make everything right. That will be a guiding light for them. The time for me to set you free is near. I will soon save you. My powerful arm will make everything right again among the nations. The islands will put their hope in me. They will wait for my powerful arm to act. (Isaiah 51:2-5)

Tempted? Run! Like David Did

In response to Pastors preaching about temptation, my oldest shouted in the silence of the church "Run, like David did." That is the response we need to give to times of temptation. It is not easy, but the Lord always provides a way of escape. May my eyes be open that I may never miss it.

Why are you so angry? The LORD asked Cain. Why do you look so dejected? You will be accepted if you do what is right. But if you refuse to do what is right, then watch out! Sin is crouching at the door, eager to control you. But you must subdue it and be its master.
One-day Cain suggested to his brother, "Let's go out into the fields." And while they were in the field, Cain attacked his brother, Abel, and killed him. Genesis 4:8

When Trouble Strikes

Often when troubles strike, we don't understand the Lord's purpose for it in our lives. I reflect on Our Daily Bread's reading that shared the issues that the Hall-of- Faith-ers experienced....:

Job got the starring role in a cosmic tragedy. His crime? He was blameless and upright (Job 1:8). Joseph, falsely accused of attempted rape, languished in prison for years—to serve God's good purposes (Gen. 39:19–41:1). And Jeremiah was beaten and put in stocks (Jer. 20:2). What was the prophet's offense? Telling the truth to rebellious people (Jer. 26:15).

Today whatever you're going through, know that God remains in control. Stand firm. Keep the faith.

Say to those with fearful hearts, "Be strong, do not fear; your God will come, he will come with vengeance; with divine retribution he will come to save you." (Isaiah 35:4)

Trapped

Ever been driving and caught between truck and heavy traffic with nowhere to turn on either side? Yet, suddenly just as you get the opportunity to overtake, the truck veers into the next lane leaving you right where you started—behind the truck. Then you must fight the battle to get back in the other lane.

That's how it is with God when He tries to teach us. All we need is a little patience until the way becomes clear. But our human frailties keep us trying to help ourselves. Let's let go and let God have His way.

For the vision is yet for an appointed time, but at the end it shall speak, and not lie: though it tarry, wait for it; because it will surely come, it will not tarry. (Habakkuk 2:3)

Restoration

Out great big wonderful God is almighty. He heals and restores the broken-hearted. He calms, gives confidence, leads, guides, protects, and comforts. He speaks to the wind and the waves, and they obey Him. Our God is divine.

Lord strengthen our faith. Help us to trust you with all of life's problems. Give us your peace despite our human frailties and turmoil.

He got up, rebuked the wind and said to the waves, "Quiet! Be still!" Then the wind died down and it was completely calm. He said to his disciples, "Why are you so afraid? Do you still have no faith?" (Mark 4:39-40)

The Simple Unexpected Solution

Ever been going through stuff? You pray to the Lord, then expect His response to be in some big way; yet His answer comes in a simple solution. We then hesitate, question, and procrastinate. All because we expected Him to ask us to do some big thing.

But that is not how our God works. He often answers in a still small voice that may even be missed if we are not attentive. This is what happened to Naaman. But when in humility he listened and obeyed, he was cleansed.

Lord help me to be open to the simple solutions; to be attentive to hear your answers to my prayers. For when I am weak, you are strong.

She said to her mistress, "If only my master would see the prophet who is in Samaria! He would cure him of his leprosy." Naaman's servants went to him and said, "My father, if the prophet had told you to do some great thing, would you not have done it? How much more, then, when he tells you, 'Wash and be cleansed'. 2King 5:3-2Kgs 5:13

Jesus Does the Unexpected

He spat on the blind man's eyes and healed him. He told him to dip in the dirty water, and he was healed. He led the children of Israel to the Red Sea (that looked like certain peril), but then He did the miraculous and parted it, and they were saved. And there are many more examples.

Lord help me to trust you even when things don't make sense 'humanly.'

But when you ask, you must believe and not doubt, because the one who doubts is like a wave of the sea, blown and tossed by the wind. (James 1:6)

Purpose of Trials

Trials come in many forms. God wants us, but the purpose remains the same. God wants us to rise above them, persevere through them, and emerge stronger than them. Hold firm. Keep strong.

Though He slay me yet will I Trust Him. (Job 13:15)

This Too Shall Pass

O- the nice thing about valleys is that there is an end to them. No matter how dark it seems, there is a time when it will end, and you will break into sunshine. Yes, as you work today, hold on, knowing that this too will pass.

For our light and momentary troubles are achieving for us an eternal glory that far outweighs them all. 18 So we fix our eyes not on what is seen, but on what is unseen, since what is seen is temporary, but what is unseen is eternal. (2 Corinthians 4:17-18)

Trying Times

Paul wrote Philemon, Philippians, Ephesians, and Colossians while imprisoned. My GreenLight content was written during the most trying time of my life. I guess it could only have been written at those times. When I do not understand the troubles in life, my Heavenly Father does. I have concluded to forever trust His plans for me for He has it all under control.

"I'm not saying that because I need anything. I have learned to be content no matter what happens to me." – Philippians 4:11

Use What God Has Given You

Remember to use what God has given you in your hand. Could it be educating, landscaping, encouraging, corporate training, your network? Just use what God has given you and receive His gifts that He has provided to meet your needs.

Remember to Ask, seek, knock, and the door will be opened sooner than you think because the Lord Himself will answer. Be bold. Go ahead and face your fears!

For the Spirit God gave us does not make us timid, but gives us power, love and self-discipline. (2 Timothy 1:7)

Victory is Mine

God's grace is sufficient, and He assures me that victory is mine. I can bask in the knowledge that He's got everything under control.

Jesus looked at them and said, "With man this is impossible, but with God all things are possible." (Mathew 19:26)

When You Don't Understand

When you don't understand continue to trust in the Lord with all your heart and not lean on your own understanding of what makes sense. Acknowledge the Lord in everything. Ask Him to direct you in your decisions; in your walk; in your lack of understanding of where He wants you to go, what He wants you to do; and to wait on Him to show or tell you how He wants you to do what He wants you to do.

Because of the Lord's great love we are not consumed, for his compassions never fail. They are new every morning; great is your faithfulness. I say to myself, The Lord is my portion; therefore I will wait for him. (Lamentations 3:22-24)

Where are You, Lord?

Where are you, Lord? Where are you? I need your help right now—today. Lord, can you not see that I am about to drown in my needs that will cause me embarrassment and shame? I am like the disciples in the boat when everything seemed hopeless, and they were about to drown. But you came through immediately, and supernaturally. Lord show me—no don't show me—just do your thing supernaturally right now.

Holy Spirit, please grant me hope. Please grant me faith. Please refresh my inner spirit with your peace that passes all understanding. So as the daily bread said, In the face of fear, we need to hear Jesus ask, "Why are you fearful?" and be reminded that He will never leave you nor forsake you. There is nothing that He can't overcome and therefore nothing for you to fear.

So, today as you are haunted by your fears when the problems seem too mountainous to overcome in your own strength, remember that you can rely on Jesus, your fearless Champion.

Lord, thank you for the reminder that you will never leave me nor forsake me. When I am afraid, I know that I can rely on your presence and power to calm my heart and overcome my fears. In times of fear, call out to Jesus, our fearless Champion.

God has said, Never will I leave you; never will I forsake you. (Hebrews 13:5)

Your Eye is on the Sparrow

I know He watches over me. People think I'm crazy to trust the Lord in the midst of my sorrows, pain and deep sadness, but it's all I know to do. He has brought me through sad circumstances before, and I know He will do it again.

What do I do when I don't know what to do? I will try Jesus. I will pray, cry and thank him because I'm confident that all things work together for good to those who love the Lord. I love him and therefore trust that this battle that I'm going through now will pass. He will see me through because I trust only him because it's for my good. How can this shame, embarrassment be for my good? Only God knows. I am weak Lord; please give me the strength to hold on for as long as it takes even though it seems like an eternity. Come through today Lord as only you can. For this I thank you.

Are not two sparrows sold for a penny? Yet not one of them will fall to the ground outside your Father's care. And even the very hairs of your head are all numbered. 31 So don't be afraid; you are worth more than many sparrows. (Matthew 10:29-31)

While Waiting

While waiting, be encouraged. Still do regular stuff. Remember your life can't be placed on hold. Who says tomorrow is guaranteed to you? So, stay close to God. Talk to Him. He will hold your right hand and bring you comfort while you wait.

For the vision is yet for an appointed time, but at the end it shall speak, and not lie: though it tarry, wait for it; because it will surely come, it will not tarry. (Habakkuk 2:3)

God's Will

Step-by-step; day-by-day; moment-by-moment. That's how we know God's will. He gives clarity as we need it not more. He feeds the birds of the air. In the same way, He takes care of our every need. If He were to give us more, maybe we could not handle it. Either we would gloat in our future success, or we may get overwhelmed.

Lord, please keep guiding me and give me the patience, peace, serenity, faith, and trust as I wait on you. Please take control and lead me step-by-step; day by day; moment by moment. Thank you, Jesus.

The Lord works out everything to its proper end—even the wicked for a day of disaster. (16:4)

Work Hard

Work hard. Plant seeds in different areas—in different ways. The Lord will come through soon, some way, somehow.

Sow your seed in the morning, and at evening let your hands not be idle, for you do not know which will succeed, whether this or that, or whether both will do equally well.

Whispers

God hears our whispers. But we must try. As my youngest was about to pass out from heat, hunger, and exhaustion, she whispered the name of her campsite medic. God through His amazing strength, touched the medic who came running. Only God. Only God. Yes indeed, the Lord is amazing.

For the eyes of the Lord are on the righteous and his ears are attentive to their prayer (1 Peter 3:12)

Experiencing God

While participating in an Experiencing God Bible study, this verse was profound as it was laid in my heart to record my experience a few years ago. It was the most challenging time for me when I took my teenage sophomore daughter and relocated to Maryland to finish my research.

Spiritually, it was the most astounding year of growth. I made it through holding onto Christ. I experienced everything difficult, but God had me still standing. I felt the urge through the spirit to record my spiritual journey and the collection of verse, prayers, and anecdotes that brought me through. I stepped forward in faith and learnt how to make this a reality.

It was the Lord's Day, and I was worshiping in the Spirit. Suddenly, I heard behind me a loud voice like a trumpet blast. It said, "write in a book everything you see and send it to the seven churches in the cities of Ephesus, Smyrna, Pergamum, Thyatira, Sardis, Philadelphia, and Laodicea." (Revelation 1:10-11)

Lord Use Me

Lord use me. Just like you used men of old …Daniel, Moses, Abraham, Joseph, Ruth, Esther. Lord make me willing. And when you do use me to accomplish your will, if there is any praise, Lord, please take away my pride and make me humble in the knowledge that you alone deserve the praise, honor and the glory.

Then I heard the voice of the Lord saying, "Whom shall I send? And who will go for us? And I said, "Here am I. Send me!" (Isaiah 6:8)

I Do Not Understand

I do not understand, but I do know that God's ways are not my ways. I am sure that all things work together for good. Thank you, Lord for loving me. Thank you, Lord for sustaining me. Thank you, lord for being there for me when I'm weak as I am these days. Thank you, lord for your answer to my prayers especially when I do not know what to pray. All I know is that I want your will and plan for my life. So, mold me and make me just the way you want me. This is my prayer.

As the heavens are higher than the earth, so are my ways higher than your ways and my thoughts than your thoughts. (Isaiah 55:9)

God Will Vindicate

God takes it seriously when others try to discredit you. But God sees. He hears. He understand and will vindicate you. Just be still and allow Him to fight your battle.

The Lord is a God who avenges. O God who avenges, shine forth. Rise up, Judge of the earth; pay back to the proud what they deserve. (Psalm 94:1-2)

My Way

I want to have it my way. How many times have we said that? Or maybe not said but acted that way? Lord I want this; I want that; by that date; and by that time. Lord since your way is always best; please help me to quietly and patiently wait on you.

Teach me thy way, O Lord; I will walk in thy truth: unite my heart to fear thy name. (Psalm 86:11)

At Nights When You Awake

Speak Lord, Thy Servant heareth. Sometimes at night, He wakes us up to pray as He did with Samuel. So, whenever you wake up at night, take this as an indication that He wants to hear from you. There's something He wants you to do. Take the step. Be obedient. Pray.

The LORD came and stood there, calling as at the other times, "Samuel! Samuel!" Then Samuel said, "Speak, for your servant is listening." (1 Samuel 3:10)

Wait

Be Willing to Wait, Delay Gratification. Thank you, God, for all the good things you have planned for me if I'm willing to wait.

That is why for Christ's sake, I delight in weaknesses, in insults, in hardships, in persecutions, in difficulties. For when I am weak, then I am strong. (2 Corinthians 12:10)

What if... God...

When in doubt and pondering what if—I don't get the.... Remember that God will help. Just stand still and watch Him work things out for your good. He always comes through—always.

What if God knows all my problems, cares, and concerns? What if God has everything all arranged? What if He has everything already set up and will release them at the right time as He did with the bills, mortgage, spouse, studies? What if He already has everything under His control? What if the answer is just around the corner? What if it's next week?

Then I need to be prepared.

Lord, please give me the strength to trust you more today. Give me the strength, the faith, the encouragement to wait on you knowing that all things—my concerns, aspirations, needs, desires and everything ... you will take care of for me. After all, nothing is too hard for you my God, because you are in control. We have a high priest who can feel it when we are weak and hurting.

For we do not have a high priest who is unable to empathize with our weaknesses, but we have one who has been tempted in every way, just as we are—yet he did not sin. Let us then approach God's throne of grace with confidence, so that we may receive mercy and find grace to help us in our time of need. (Hebrews 4:15-16)

Wait Expectantly

Waiting expectantly on the Lord's answer to our prayer. He is able, and He will come through. You can be confident of that.

The Lord will provide His guiding presence as we wait patiently for Him to bring about His will. Tune your anxious heart to patience, walk by faith where sight is dim. Be calm and trustful, and leave everything to Him. —Chambers

Out of the depths I cry to you, Lord; Lord, hear my voice. Let your ears be attentive to my cry for mercy. I wait for the Lord, my whole being waits, and in his word, I put my hope. (Psalm 130:1, 2, 5)

God is at Work

God is at work. God is working. Whichever way I may want to put it, He's up to something. Yes, He is. Just wait; just watch and see. He is up to something!

For it is God who works in you to will and to act in order to fulfill his good purpose (Philippians 2:13)

What Lies Ahead

With God behind you and His arms beneath you, you can face whatever lies ahead of you.

They said to Moses, "Was it because there were no graves in Egypt that you brought us to the desert to die? What have you done to us by bringing us out of Egypt? Didn't we say to you in Egypt, 'Leave us alone; let us serve the Egyptians'? It would have been better for us to serve the Egyptians than to die in the desert!" (Exodus 14:11-12)

Wisdom

If you want wisdom, ask. Dear God, give me wisdom today.

If any of you lacks wisdom, you should ask God, who gives generously to all without finding fault, and it will be given to you (James 1:5)

Prayer: 6 Years Ago

No, it's not what you're thinking. My grandson RJ when I asked him to pray for me said he did— 6 years ago At least he was honest even though he was only 4 years old at the time.

How many times have we asked someone to pray for us? Often, they forget. May we take the time out to pray for someone in need today.

After Job had prayed for his friends, the Lord restored his fortunes and gave him twice as much as he had before. (Job 42:10)

New Year. Renewed Trust

Lord in the New Year take my hands, my feet, my thoughts and my speech, make them all yours. Work through me in all that I do. Go ahead of me, take your will and make it mine. And Lord if I object; if I am afraid, give me the courage to trust that you are in control. With that grant me peace. Peace in lack. Peace in confusion. Peace when I don't know what to do. Peace when I can't find my way. Lord grant me wisdom, love and understanding and above all, patience.

For the vision is yet for an appointed time; But at the end it will speak, and it will not lie. Though it tarries, wait for it; Because it will surely come, it will not tarry. (Habakkuk 2:3)

Prepped

Before God blesses us, He prepares us for the blessing.

Elisha said, "Go around and ask all your neighbors for empty jars. Don't ask for just a few. Then go inside and shut the door behind you and your sons. Pour oil into all the jars, and as each is filled, put it to one side." (2 Kings 4:3-4)

Savior of the World

Dialogue during devotion with my one-and-two-year-old grandsons' RJ and Xavier: Mary had baby Jesus, and He became the Savior of the world. Annoyed RJ retorts; "Xavier is the 'Xavior' of the world? What about RJ?"

Jealousy at such a young age. Indeed, we are born in iniquity and sin.

Surely, I was sinful at birth, sinful from the time my mother conceived me. (Psalm 51:5)

Worry

Do not worry. Our heavenly Father knows that what we need even before we ask. So be comforted. Remember the popular chorus, if you know the Lord is keeping you, what are you going to worry about? Bask in the confidence that what the Lord has said, He will do.

Cast your cares on the LORD and he will sustain you; he will never let the righteous be shaken. (Psalm 55:22)

Let It Be a Yes

Whatever God's promises, they are yes in Christ Jesus.

Sovereign Lord, you are God! Your covenant is trustworthy, and you have promised these good things to your servant. Now be pleased to bless the house of your servant, that it may continue forever in your sight; for you, Sovereign Lord, have spoken, and with your blessing the house of your servant will be blessed forever. (2 Samuel 7:28, 29)

A Time for Everything

There is a time for everything and a season for every activity under the heavens.

He has made everything beautiful in its time. He has also set eternity in the human heart; yet no one can fathom what God has done from beginning to end. (Ecclesiastes 3:11)

About The Author

Dr. Shelly Cameron is an Organizational Leadership Specialist. Through her book **Success Strategies of Immigrant Leaders,** she revealed the results of a Phenomenological study conducted with Nova Southeastern University and published in the Journal of American Academy of Business Cambridge (JAABC) which explored the hidden secrets of successful leaders. She now connects it to those aspiring to achieve. Individuals are challenged to take that first step to accomplish their dreams, goals, and aspirations. As Author, Speaker, and Coach, Dr. Cameron holds Graduate degrees in Organizational Leadership, Health Administration, and Human Resource Development.

An avid believer in Prayer, Dr. Cameron has traveled as far as Kenya, East Africa on Missions to share her Passion for Prayer and its link to Personal Development.

She holds firmly to the stance that All Things Are Possible with God.

If You Have Enjoyed This Book

Or If It Has Touched Your Life In Some Way, I would Love to Hear from You.

Please email me at:

scameron@ccahr.com

www.shellycameron.com

Books By Dr. Shelly Cameron

GreenLight: When God Says Go

Motivational Quotes To Boost Your Success

Success Strategies: Want To Succeed? Here's How

Success Strategies of Immigrant Leaders in The United States

Success Strategies of Caribbean American Leaders in the United States: Why Some Succeed While Others Don't

The Leadership Challenge (JAABC) Business Journal

www.ingramcontent.com/pod-product-compliance
Lightning Source LLC
Chambersburg PA
CBHW051938290426
44110CB00015B/2022